Saving Catholic Marriages

Living Your Legacy of Love

Alberta K. Pizzitola
Gary V. Pizzitola, Ph.D.

NIHIL OBSTAT   Rev. Monsignor Peter D. Bui
                Theological Consultant and Priest
                Assistant to the Bishop

IMPRIMATUR   + Thomas J. Olmsted
                Bishop of Phoenix, Arizona
                August 14, 2020

All scriptural passages have been taken from The Holy Bible, Revised Standard Version, Second Catholic Edition, Copyright 2006, Division of Christian Education of the National Council of the Churches of Christ in the United States of America.

For Catechism: All passages have been taken from the Catechism of the Catholic Church, Second Edition for the United States of America, Copyright 1994, United States Catholic Conference, Inc. English translation of the Catechism of the Catholic Church: Modifications from the Editio Typica, Copyright 1997, United States Catholic Conference, Inc. — Libreria Editrice Vaticana.

Saving Catholic Marriages: Living Your Legacy of Love

Published by Holy Catholic Marriage LLC
Phoenix, Arizona

ISBN: 978-0-578-76573-0 (paperback)
ISBN: 978-0-578-76574-7 (ebook)

LCCN: 2020918056

Peace Prayer
of Saint Francis

Lord, make me an instrument of your peace:
where there is hatred, let me sow love;
where there is injury, pardon;
where there is doubt, faith;
where there is despair, hope;
where there is darkness, light;
where there is sadness, joy.

O divine Master, grant that I may not so much seek
to be consoled as to console,
to be understood as to understand,
to be loved as to love.
For it is in giving that we receive,
it is in pardoning that we are pardoned,
and it is in dying that we are born to eternal life.
Amen.

Dedication

We dedicate this labor of love to our children, our grandchildren and all future generations.

May they continue to live the LEGACY OF LOVE began so many years ago by our parents and all the faithful Catholics in previous generations of our families, guided always by their strong faith and love of God, remaining ever faithful to Jesus and the Church He founded on His Apostles.

Table of Contents

Preface

Gary and I came from intact, practicing Catholic homes founded on a love of the Catholic faith and family, raised by parents who were devoted to each other. But, we found marriage to be difficult. Although Gary had three degrees in psychology, together with a great deal of training in marital therapy and I had a degree in sociology, neither of us really understood Catholic teaching about marriage. I attended daily Mass, taught religious education and prayed a daily rosary. Even so, we were not exempt from acquiring certain aspects of our secular, godless culture. We had forgotten that our marriage was a Sacrament of the Catholic Church. We were bound together in Christ's love but were not living Christ's love for each other.

I would love to say that once we realized we were a Sacrament we changed but that was not the case. Actually, we were on the brink of divorce. Gary's anger, learned from his family of origin, was destroying me and I was unable to forgive him. In addition, we were very focused on materialism. Gary worked long hours paying for our lifestyle which increased his anger and my lack of forgiving. We finally reached the breaking point; I could no longer remain married. As I plotted my first move to leave, God struck me with a vivid flashback of my wedding day, leading to a very real conversation with Him. There we were, dressed in our wedding finery at my Catholic church with Jesus present in His golden tabernacle, the altar of His sacrifice ready for Holy Mass. I watched this interior vision of Gary and I pledging our vows to God and each other. It was a riveting experience that I have reflected on many times. Through my tears I said, "Okay, Jesus, I'm listening. I'll turn to you. Show me how to love my husband as he needs to be loved." And He did. I then heard the interior voice tell me my "mission field" was sitting downstairs with a broken heart. Please understand this was not me talking to myself. The last thing in the world I wanted to do was go downstairs and make things right! It was my moment of truth. Did I love God enough to swallow my pride and make my marriage right? Was I willing to listen and obey Him?

Dedicating ourselves to a year of weekly reconciliation and daily rosary, our wounds healed. We are still far from perfect but have a newfound, growing intimacy and are happier than we ever expected. That was twenty-five years ago.

Having walked through the fire of a painful marriage and having a new understanding of spiritual warfare, Gary and I began preparing couples for marriage in the Diocese of Phoenix. Soon after, we began mentoring married couples struggling with the many issues confronting today's Catholic, sacramental marriages, focusing on living one's love for both God and spouse, the importance of growing in the faith, the Sacraments, couple prayer and developing practical strategies and skills to deal with the many issues confronting Catholic marriages and families.

Six years ago, I began to write stories of couples we were working with living ongoing, painful experiences. Gary would often ask, "What are you writing and what are you going to do with it all?" Each entry was a story, free flowing from actual experiences with couples. This book is the compilation of some of those stories, experiences, suggestions and strategies. What we have realized is that God's plan was for us to walk through the fire of our difficulties in order to help other Catholic couples live their faith and grow in their love for God and each other.

Saving Catholic Marriages is not *just* a book. Rather, it is a process and vehicle for real change in marriage . . . your marriage. If possible, read the chapters as a couple, discuss them and make use of the suggestions offered. Please use the suggestions of prayer, sacrificial love, service and Sacraments. The goal is for spouses to learn to grow in love and holiness through the Sacraments Jesus offers us through His Church. As each couple grows closer to God, they will grow closer to each other and as they grow in their service and sacrificial love for each other, their children will learn the *legacy of love* God has given us.

If you are "alone" in your marriage, there are suggestions for you too and yes, change is possible!

Introduction

Picture this: you are buckled in your seat on an airplane, bags stowed, ready to go. Then, the captain's voice comes on the PA announcing there is a 66% chance the flight will crash! "What did he say?" You look up at the flight crew and they are getting off the plane. You look at the other passengers who have been immersed in their electronics. Suddenly, they realize what they just heard and begin shouting, "What? What's he saying?" Call buttons are being pushed and the once quiet passengers are frantically gathering up their belongings, rushing to get off the plane!

What does a story about airplanes have to do with a book about Catholic marriage?

Would you board a plane knowing these disturbing statistics? I doubt it. Yet, Catholic marriages are crashing and burning at an alarming rate. The disturbing statistics from the American Association of Marital and Family Therapy report the national divorce rate at 66% for first marriages and 72% for second marriages! In addition, 70% of American children live with only one biological parent! For Catholic marriages, the numbers are nearly identical and illustrate the difficulty in establishing and maintaining healthy marriages.

Marriage preparation begins in one's family of origin. Children learn what they live. Those from broken marriages have not seen their parents willing to work together to change toxic habits and create a peaceful, loving marriage. They have not seen their parents work together through difficult issues and emerge wiser and more in love. One of a child's most important life lessons is to experience the decision of their parents' determination to learn to love each other despite painful difficulties. Instead, 70% of American children experience the sorrow of failed love, failed marriages and broken homes. As young adults, they attend friends' weddings who seem so much in love on that special day, only to learn years later their love was really lust and fun masquerading as love and that it was not strong enough to last. They reason lifelong love and commitment is not a reality and divorce is simply part of the normal process of life. It is a vicious cycle Satan perpetuates as he tries to ensnare mankind in disappointment and discouragement, promoting the lies that if God is love and love does not last then both God and love are illusions.

Marriage is to reflect Jesus' sacrificial love for His Bride, the Church. The sacrificial love that is required in a sacramental marriage between one man and one woman can only come from Jesus, for He is the source of faithful, fruitful love and forgiveness born of merciful love for His Church. So, the true concept of marriage is to be found only in Jesus and His Church where He binds a husband and wife together with His powerful, sacramental graces to endure the stresses and difficulties of life. Because Jesus is love, we go to Him when we lack love, so He can transfuse us with His divine love and life in the Sacraments.

The ideal wedding day is one in which the newly wedded spouses love each other the least. What? Why? Because they have yet to weather the storms of life. As the anniversaries pass, they will endure suffering but create a history of compromise, unselfish love, mutual effort and the willingness to help each other carry their crosses . . . this is love tested just as gold is tested in fire. A tested love is a true love, while promised love is yet to be seen or tested. For centuries, Catholic couples have succeeded in living their love for each other despite poverty, persecutions, deaths, famines and wars. Their marriages remained intact because husband and wife depended on each other for their survival and that of their children. Of course, there was suffering and loss but they remained together and their love for each other grew and became stronger with each passing year. Today, we live in a privileged time of plenty where people choose not to love. It is hard work to love; it is so much easier to hold onto one's selfishness.

Love is an action word that will be tested like gold in fire. Love must be lived daily to survive all the attacks of Satan. Serving our beloved when we are tired, mad or just do not feel like it can be a struggle. But, with sacramental grace and remembering Jesus is present in every moment, we can place our spouse's needs before our own with a joyful heart. The goal is to learn to love our spouse more than ourselves as we grow in intimacy through the years, celebrating anniversaries and finding ourselves more in love than we could have imagined on our wedding day. However, to achieve this living love requires dedication and determination to follow a set of priorities. Living our love by living the priorities will lead to a special intimacy between husband and wife.

The following are the priorities of a healthy, happy, holy Catholic marriage. Live them daily, pray daily as a couple and rely on the Sacraments given by Jesus to grow in grace. You will then live the kind of marriage Jesus desires.

The Five Priorities:

1. To Live Our Love for God
2. To Live Our Love for Our Spouse
3. To Live Our Love for Our Children
4. Work
5. Everything Else

When we first started working with couples in marriage, the priorities were more simply written: God, Spouse, Children, Work, Everything Else. However, in preparing couples in which a Catholic was marrying a person of no religion, one who was agnostic or who had been so secularized that they knew nothing about God, they would say, "Sure, God can be first." However, their concept of God was often nonexistent. He was an idea on a cloud somewhere or just some tough guy with a ton of rules. So, we changed our first three priorities to more accurately reflect Jesus' two great Commandments of love. We are to love God actively with our whole mind, heart and strength and to love our neighbor as our self. Our point? God is not an idea but a pure and real Spirit. He is three Persons in one God: The Blessed Trinity. Love is not just some sentimental, romantic idea. Love is tough stuff lived out in determination when life is hard. It is the keeping of a covenant made before God. It is a decision made in the depths of our being and soul that proclaims, "I'll love you no matter what." Living the priorities will bring truth, peace and love into your lives, clearing the confusion and chaos of the world's lies, distractions and distortions.

Living Your Legacy of Love

Legacy: a gift or bequest that is handed down, endowed or conveyed from one person to another; something one comes into possession of that is transmitted, inherited or received from an ancestor or predecessor.

Legacies are usually material items such as real estate, stocks, bonds, money or jewelry. Because they are material, they are left behind. However, there is one legacy that transcends this life which can grow with each generation and be taken with us to heaven: the *legacy of love.*

God's legacy of divine love is the true legacy. He gave us His divine image, imprinting our souls to love as He loves. God's legacy continued in His gift to us of His only Son, Jesus, true Man and true God who taught us how to love through prayer and the Sacraments.

Each of us is responsible to live the true legacy of love in our sacramental marriage. By openly living our love, we will teach this legacy to our children and their children. Living our love through selfless, sacrificial service will precede us as a beacon of light to heaven.

Your marriage is *Your Legacy of Love.*

Pass it on!

Sacred Oath

The word "Sacrament" means "Sacred Oath."

Throughout the centuries, warriors of undying loyalty were trained and tested to endure the pain and hardship of battle. These warriors took a sacred oath to king and kingdom and lived out their oath in heroic love until death.

On our wedding day, we also took a sacred oath, one that is binding and eternal. As the soldiers of centuries past, we too are called upon to live out our "Sacred Oath" or "Sacrament." Our circumstances can become difficult as our spouse becomes a cross for us to bear and almost impossible to love as our sacred duty requires. However, our Sacrament will remain intact if we remain bound together in Jesus' presence and eternal love. It is a battle and that is why we on earth are called the Church Militant. With obedient love for the Father and merciful love for those His Son has given us to love, we will be triumphant!

The following are excerpts from the *Catechism of the Catholic Church* on the "Sacrament" of Catholic marriage:

1131. "The sacraments are efficacious* signs of grace, instituted by Christ and entrusted to the Church, by which divine life is dispensed to us. The visible rites by which the sacraments are celebrated signify and make present the graces proper to each sacrament. They bear fruit in those who receive them with the required dispositions."

1638. "From a valid marriage arises *a bond* between the spouses which by its very nature is perpetual and exclusive: furthermore, in a Christian marriage the spouses are strengthened and as it were, consecrated for the duties and the dignity of their state *by a special sacrament."*

1639. "The consent by which the spouses mutually give and receive one another is sealed by God himself. From their covenant arises "an institution, confirmed by the divine law . . . even in the eyes of society." The covenant between the spouses is integrated into God's covenant with man: "Authentic married love is caught up into divine love."

1640. "Thus *the marriage bond* has been established by God himself in such a way that a marriage concluded and consummated between baptized persons can never be dissolved. This bond, which results from the free human act of the spouses and their consummation of the marriage, is a reality, henceforth irrevocable, and gives rise to a covenant guaranteed by God's fidelity. The Church does not have the power to contravene this disposition of divine wisdom."

1641. "By reason of their state in life and their order, [Christian spouses] have their own special gifts in the People of God." This grace proper to the sacrament of Matrimony is intended to perfect the couple's love and to strengthen their indissoluble unity. By this grace they "help one another to attain holiness in their married life and in welcoming and educating their children."

1642. *Christ is the source of this grace.* "Just as of old God encountered his people with a covenant of love and fidelity, so our Savior, the spouse of the Church, now encounters Christian spouses through the sacrament of Matrimony." Christ dwells with them, gives them the strength to take up their crosses and so follow him, to rise again after they have fallen, to forgive one another, to bear one another's burdens, to "be subject to one another out of reverence for Christ," and to love one another with supernatural, tender and fruitful love. In the joys of their love and family life he gives them here on earth a foretaste of the wedding feast of the Lamb.

*efficacious: producing the effect it intended. Something efficacious is full of accomplishment. Synonyms; effective, successful, effectual, productive, fruitful, potent, powerful.

Our First Priority:

To Live Our Love for God

I

Our First Priority:
To Live Our Love for God

"But seek first His kingdom and His righteousness,
and all these things shall be yours as well" **(Mt 6:33).**

As Catholic couples desiring a holy, sacramental marriage, we are to seek God first. We are to build our marriage on Jesus and the Church He founded two thousand years ago on His Apostles, seeking to receive the sacramental graces that will help us on our journey through life. God must be the center of our lives. Only His divine providence and sacramental graces will see us through the bad and sick times of our marriage and lives. We know He is a good and gracious God who is love and who bestows love on all who seek Him. So, seeking God, His kingdom and righteousness is the obvious path to love and happiness.

However, when we seek our way first and not God's way, we begin a very difficult journey without the necessary understanding and graces to endure life's difficulties. The "our way first" attitude without the help of Jesus comes from our first parents, Adam and Eve. God gave them a perfect life and a perfect world, asking only that they obey one rule for their protection and well-being. Obedience to this one rule would have demonstrated to God, their Father, their love and appreciation. We are all aware of what happened: Satan seized his window of opportunity for destruction and our parents disobeyed God, forfeiting grace and righteousness. Sin entered the world, fracturing the relationship between God and mankind. This original sin has left all of us wounded, struggling with a flawed, fallen human nature.

Although the holy waters of baptism washed away original sin, we are still left with the effects: a darkened understanding, weakened will and an attraction to sin that can destroy even a sacramental, Catholic marriage. However, we can fight our attraction to sin by receiving the Sacraments, cooperating with their graces and continually seeking God through prayer, the Mass and the Sacrament of Reconciliation, obediently allowing Him to guide and guard our lives.

What can we learn from the story of our first parents? We are to seek God, His Kingdom and His righteousness through obedient love. God owns everything . . . except our free will. Adam and Eve gave their free will to Satan, the enemy of God and mankind. Giving God our free will brings blessings while giving Satan our free will brings sin, destruction, pain and death.

Jesus said, *"If you love me, you will keep my commandments"* (Jn 14:15). If we love Jesus, we will do as He asks. Jesus, true God and true man, reconciled man with God by His life, death and resurrection. He accepted death on a cross obediently because of His love for His Father and His merciful love for sinful mankind. When we use our free will to obey, we are like the child who says, "Yes, Daddy, I will do this because I love you so much and want to always please you." But, when we listen to the voice of our selfish, fallen nature, we misuse our free will by saying, "I will not obey you, God, because I do not love You as much as I love myself. I come first, not You."

There is no decision we will ever make that is more important than who we choose to marry. The consequences of this decision will impact not only our lives but also the lives of our children and future generations. As Catholic couples, we are faced with a hostile, secular culture, constantly enticing us to reject a belief in God and an obedience to Him, discouraging us from living lives of self-control as "too restrictive and repressive." We are encouraged to become pleasure seekers without a thought to God or the harm sin does to us and our fellow man. Sin is incredibly destructive to mankind.

We fight Satan by cooperating with sacramental grace, becoming spiritually stronger and able to judge decisions by obeying the Commandments of love as well as understanding the consequences of disobeying them. Recognize whose voice we listen to: Jesus invites us to obey and follow Him, while Satan deceives us to turn from our loving God. Life is a series of choices leading us to or away from God. We must choose wisely.

God is love and we turn to Him when we need to love. This is just common sense: we go to the market for food, the bank for money and God for love. Seeking God first and turning to Him will enable us to be the one out of every three first marriages that remain intact. We also realize seeking holiness is our purpose; God created all of us for the purpose of holy love. Making this the focus of life, we will experience a deep and radiant joy as we encounter life's many twists and turns. Sadly, many couples do not seek God to learn how to love their beloved spouse. They ignore the fact God created marriage (man did not) and that He is pure holiness and goodness (man is not). God's capacity to love is eternal, all-giving and sacrificial, as was Jesus' dying on the cross for His Bride, the Church. However, Jesus did so much more. He taught us the Kingdom of God is right here, right now when we live obediently according to His teachings. He trained twelve men to become the foundation of His Church, to continue His teachings, giving them the authority to administer sacramental grace to His Church handed down to all generations through Apostolic Succession. Sacramental grace helps us grow in holiness and combat the evil to which we are exposed. Cooperating with and accepting God's holy love and the graces available in the Sacraments strengthens weak, human love to endure all things in peace, patience and perseverance.

Remember Jesus' words about first seeking God and then all else will be given to us? Too often, we focus our attention first on the "all else" and leave God until later. Then, when life is not working well, we wonder, "Where's God in my life?" The answer is really very simple. We left Him behind, placing many other people, places and things ahead of Him. However, the great news is that it is never too late to bring Jesus back into our life, our marriage and our family. There is no better time than now to build a healthier, happier, holier Catholic marriage filled with sacramental grace.

Share this with your spouse and live your *legacy of love*. Continue to sincerely seek God, knowing you will need the powerful, sacramental graces to help you live your vows to love and honor until death. Each Sacrament has been instituted by Christ to give the needed graces, an efficacious sign that produces the desired effect or intended result it is performing. Throughout your marriage, as sacramentally married spouses, turn to God in prayer, sacrifice, service and dying to one's own selfishness, to receive ongoing graces in meeting life's every challenge.

Obedient Love

"I am the Lord your God, who brought you out of the land of Egypt, out of the house of bondage. You shall have no other gods before me . . . visiting the iniquity of the fathers upon the children to the third and fourth generation of those who hate me, but showing mercy to thousands of those who love me and keep my commandments"
(Ex 20:2, 3, 5b-6).

"Blessed are those whose way is blameless, who walk in the law of the Lord! Blessed are those who keep His testimonies, who seek Him with their whole heart" (Ps 119:1, 2).

Will your legacy as a father be obedient love of God and selfless love for spouse and children? A father's behavior—good or bad—affects their immediate family as well as future genera-tions. Behaviors have consequences and those consequences can permeate many generations. Remember the old saying about life not being a dress rehearsal? The truth is, it is not a rehearsal but the real deal and the audience is God and family! There have been thousands of examples of fathers' good and bad behaviors throughout history as well as the impact of those behaviors on society, their children and future generations. Now, it is your turn as a father to live your love for God through obedience to Him and self-sacrificing love for your family.

The obedient love of a father who teaches his family to love God will have His blessing that reaches to a thousand generations. However, the disobedient father will leave a path of destructive sin from one generation to the next, each generation learning destructive behaviors from fathers and grandfathers. Genera-tional sin consumes families in pain and sorrow with alcoholism, drugs, violence, physical and emotional abuse. Sin passing from one generation to the next is an important concept for all of us to understand. Too many times, a father decides to do what he wants, when he wants and fails to realize their sins' far reaching effects on their children and future generations.

THE TEN COMMANDMENTS

1. I am the Lord your God. You shall not have strange gods before me.
2. You shall not take the name of the Lord your God in vain.
3. Remember to keep holy the Sabbath day.
4. Honor your father and your mother.
5. You shall not kill.
6. You shall not commit adultery.
7. You shall not steal.

8. You shall not bear false witness against your neighbor.

9. You shall not covet your neighbor's wife.

10. You shall not covet your neighbor's goods.

The Ten Commandments are based on love of God and neighbor. When obeyed they bring peace, love and joy. Jesus said, *"A new commandment I give to you, that you love one another; even as I have loved you, that you also love one another. By this all men will know that you are my disciples, if you have love for one another"* (Jn 13:34-35). Jesus lived His love for mankind by His life of sacrificial service and His obedient death on the cross. Looking at a crucifix, we can see the love Jesus has for all of us.

These are the laws of love. Loving God and our neighbor will bring peace to individuals, families and society. God is a loving Father who wants His children to obey Him, not for His benefit but for ours. He wants us to treat others with love and respect as we are all made in His divine image and are all children of the Father and brothers and sisters of Jesus. God desires us to be safe and secure; if all would obey these laws of love, society would exist without crime.

In St. Mark's Gospel (12:28-33), when Jesus was asked which was the greatest Commandment, He replied that the first was to love God with all our heart, soul, mind and strength and the second was to love our neighbor as our self. These are the two great commandments of love that Catholic couples must set their hearts on, living their love for each other, teaching them to their children. As a Church, we make sacrifices during Lent but hearing that obedience to these two laws of love is more important than offerings and sacrifices, we must understand the power and importance of obedience to God. Obedience is what God desires from us but it is not always what He receives.

Parents who live obedient love of God and teach the importance of doing so to their children, will help them grow in wisdom and discernment. This will equip them with the ability to judge behaviors and the consequences that follow with clarity to understand right from wrong and good from bad. Righteous wisdom is accepting God's laws of love to guide and protect children from those who would try to seduce them into sin. The wages or consequences of sin is death. No one wants death for their child. We have a living, loving God who wants us, His children, to make holy decisions and have an abundant life of love.

When Satan constantly tempts us with sin, we must run to the Sacrament of Reconciliation and humbly ask for the strength and graces necessary to reject the temptation and sin. Breaking God's Commandments will result in a difficult, painful marriage and life but following them will result in a happier, healthier, holier life. God blesses obedience. It is that simple!

> **Jesus obeyed.**
> **Satan did not obey.**

Share this with your spouse and live your *legacy of love*. What will your legacy be for your children? Will they be blessed for a thousand generations because of your obedient love for God or will they be punished for three or four generations because of your rebelling against Him? Be obedient to the Commandments for yourself, your spouse, your children and all your future generations.

Remembering Cana

"His mother said to the servants, do whatever He tells you" (Jn 2:5).

In Scripture, we are witnesses to one of the most famous weddings in human history. It was not a royal wedding, extensively covered by the press, nor was it televised worldwide. It was a simple, humble wedding in the tiny village of Cana, where two families came together to celebrate their children's marriage. The festivities were in full swing and there was great rejoicing at the joining of the couple and their families. Long preparation had taken place leading up to this very important day. Among the invited guests was Mary, her Son Jesus and His disciples. No one really knew Him as His time had not yet come.

At this wedding in Cana, the guests were enjoying the good food and wine when the wine steward saw the wine had run out. This was a terrible social slight to all who were gathered and would become an everlasting embarrassment to the wedding couple and their families. They had an unforeseen problem that only a miracle could remedy. The bride and groom and their families had done their best planning for this big day, serving the best wine they could afford and believing there would be enough for all. Unfortunately, they miscalculated and the wine ran out. Mary, the mother of Jesus, became aware of the shortage of wine and instructed the wine steward to do as Jesus said. Jesus ordered the waiters to fill the six stone water jars to the brim with water. He then instructed them to draw some out and take it to the wine steward. Upon tasting the miraculous wine, the steward exclaimed, *"Every man serves the good wine first; and when men have drunk freely, then the poor wine; but you have kept the good wine till now"* (Jn 2:10). Of course, Jesus always brings what is good to a wedding and marriage!

Catholic couples desiring a wedding in the Catholic Church engage in several steps of preparation including interviews and classes. Almost all possess great love for each other and are very willing to pledge their love before God, family and friends. However, a few are stubborn and certain they know better than a two-thousand-year-old Church about how to have a lasting love and marriage. They have their own idea about love and how marriage is to be lived, mistakenly believing they are in control. After years of tears, they learn their way was not good enough to withstand the difficulties they encountered because they refused to do "whatever Jesus asked of them."

Too frequently, secularized Catholic couples invite Jesus to the wedding but leave Him at the door of the church as they exit for the reception. They used the church for its beauty and then move on. Their plan is to live their busy lives without Jesus in their relationship. They do not realize how much better and less stressful their marriage and life will be if they would invite Him home with them. Catholic couples receive sacramental graces at their wedding but they must have faith and open hearts to receive the graces. Jesus is a gentleman. He does not push His way into a closed and hard heart. We must invite Him in and listen to Him through Church teaching found in Sacred Scripture and by obeying the Commandments of love.

Many brides and grooms get caught up in the festivities of the wedding celebration and forget there is a life to be lived in peace and undying love after the big day. To have a healthy, happy and holy marriage that will last, we need to follow certain steps. The first is to invite Jesus to the ceremony. He needs to be an integral part of our marriage. Jesus' presence allows Him to guide and direct us to be holy, Catholic spouses. The second step is to learn from the wine steward at Cana. He identified the problem and asked Mary, the mother of Jesus, for help. Mary always points to her Divine Son and says, "Do whatever He tells you." The third step is to listen and trust Jesus when He tells us to love with patient humility. We listen to Jesus in the frequent reception of the Sacraments and in personal and couple prayer. He tells us to be loving and forgiving even when our spouse is not loving or lovable and even when we do not feel like it. Last of all, we are to obey Jesus by doing what He says. No matter how difficult the situation in a marriage, the only answer is Jesus. When couples are humble by not insisting on their own way, willing to die to self for their beloved, always remembering their vows to love and honor, they will receive the love of Jesus in their Sacrament.

At Cana, Jesus' presence at the wedding was to bestow His miraculous, divine grace on the trouble at hand, turning plain water into abundant, exquisite wine. So too does Jesus' presence in a sacramental marriage turn the simple love of a husband and wife into abundant, exquisite and lasting love. Jesus is love. He came to teach us how to love in all circumstances. Human love is fragile and fails frequently but divine love never fails. When Jesus is part of our marriage, His divine plan will provide the sacramental graces that will help us through the good times and bad that lay ahead. It was no accident that Jesus' first miracle was to help a marriage. Everything flows from the holy union of one man and one woman, bound together in the unbreakable bond of Jesus' love. All sacramentally married couples can learn from the wine steward who obeyed Jesus when told to fill the jars with water. His lack of understanding and possible fear of serving water did not stop his obedience to Jesus. By trusting and obeying, the steward earned a privileged place in biblical history, witnessing Jesus' first great miracle which continues to be celebrated two thousand years later.

The wine of our love can run out in very difficult situations. Human love is weak. Discouragement and disappointment mount over the years causing misperceptions and misunderstandings. Destructive behaviors including addictions and infidelity can destroy a marriage. When this happens, we must remember that the love of Jesus and the Sacraments of the Church are far more powerful than our sins and problems. Nothing is more powerful than Jesus' faithful love and His sacramental graces given to His Church. It is at these times we are to turn to Jesus in the Sacrament of Reconciliation and the Eucharist to ask for and be granted the sacramental graces to love, forgive and continue with patient endurance. Jesus always provides the necessary strength and graces to live our love just as He provided the exquisite wine at

Cana. His perfect love is always renewing and healing hearts that are open to receiving His graces in the Sacraments.

Share this with your spouse and live your *legacy of love*. Is Jesus the first priority in your marriage? Do you sometimes forget He is present? Do you want a marriage that will endure? Do you understand the importance of personal prayer, couple prayer and the Sacraments? Intimacy grows when couples undress their hearts and souls in couple prayer by sharing the innermost thoughts and desires of their heart openly with God and spouse. Scripture says pray without ceasing. Begin to have a running dialogue with Jesus who resides in and speaks to your heart and soul. If you have been away from the Sacrament of Reconciliation for a time, seek God to clean out that which is hurting your soul and marriage. Intentionally deciding to be married in the Catholic Church allows Jesus to be a lasting part of your marriage. Living your love in good times and bad and loving and honoring your spouse requires open hearts for Jesus' grace to keep your marriage healthy, happy and holy. What will your legacy be? A life of love or the death of your marriage?

Focused on God

"Unless the Lord builds the house, those who build it labor in vain. Unless the Lord watches over the city, the watchman stays awake in vain" (Ps 127).

Who built our house? Was the architect capable, dependable, trustworthy? Who has been guarding our house and precious family? Are they strong, vigilant?

God created marriage and Jesus raised it to a Sacrament at Cana. But, when secularism swept the minds and hearts of our culture in the 1960's, people fired the Divine Creator and decided they would build their own houses, marriages and families. The consequences? Two out of every three first marriages ending in

SAVING CATHOLIC MARRIAGES

divorce, the breakdown of the family and subsequent breakdown of the culture. Obviously, we need God to build our houses, lives and marriages. Marriage is hard work and a healthy, holy one is impossible without God. Sadly, three generations have been raised without the slightest knowledge of God and His plan of love.

Do we love God? Does He know we love Him? What proof can we offer that will show our love for Him? Too frequently people say, "Yeah, of course I love God. I'm a good person." However, when asked about prayer, Mass or obedience to the Ten Commandments they say, "Well, this is a different age now, believing isn't the same and besides, I'm very busy." These answers may not work well when we meet Jesus face to face and instead of hearing, "Enter my Father's house, good and faithful servant," we hear, "I do not know you."

Gifted with God's divine image and free will, we have the capability for a loving relationship with our good and gracious Creator and Father. Although Adam and Eve had mistrusted and disobeyed God, He did not "smote" them because He loved them. They were the pinnacle of His beautiful creation. Throughout Old Testament history, great Kings, patriarchs and prophets would turn to God for a relationship but sin would creep into their lives and hearts and they would turn away. Over and over mankind showed His lack of love for the all good and gracious God who wanted a relationship with Him built on obedient love.

God sent His Son, Jesus, to reconcile mankind to Himself. Jesus announced the Kingdom of God was at hand. For three years He trained the Apostles how to carry on His work, telling them, *"I am the way, and the truth, and the life; no one comes to the Father, but by me. If you had known me, you would have known my Father also; henceforth you know him and have seen him." Philip said to him, "Lord, show us the Father and we will be satisfied." Jesus said to him, "Have I been with you so long, and yet you do not know me, Philip? He who has seen me has seen the Father; how can you say, 'Show us the Father?' Do you not believe that I am in the Father and the Father is in me? The words that I say to you I do not speak on my own authority; but the Father who dwells in me does His works"* (Jn 14:6-10).

Only Jesus could reconcile man with God through His obedient and sacrificial death on a cross. By His death, He gave mankind the opportunity to know God in the most personal of ways. Throughout the ages, His Apostles have passed down the divine life of Jesus found in the Sacraments so that all who believed in Him and the power of His sacramental graces would grow in holiness.

Satan's trickery worked with our first parents and he continues to use the same tactics of deceit and treachery on each of us. Remember the cartoon with the little white angel on one shoulder and little red devil on the other? While amusing, it does have a ring of truth to it: the white angel urging us to obey God's Commandments and the red devil urging us to disobey. How many times have we heard an inner voice telling us, "Come on you can do this . . . no one will know . . . you deserve this . . . it will be a good thing?" Continuing his trickery after we sin, Satan would have us believe we are worthless: "You're so bad and wicked. God will never love or forgive you for what you have done." From an initial sense of curiosity, we are now engulfed with shame and guilt, feeling terrible and unloved by God. Satan lies; he has no truth in him. We can learn from Eve's encounter by staying away from temptation and remaining aware of sins that are enticing and attractive. When we fall prey listening to the wrong voice, it is time to change channels: turn to prayer and run to Jesus in the Sacrament of Reconciliation. Building our house on sacramental grace to defend it from Satan as he rages spiritual war against us is imperative.

We are a post-Christian, secular culture. God is no longer the builder and protector of our homes. We have ushered Him out of our schools, removed the Ten Commandments from court houses and allowed schools and universities to teach error to our children. We are a culture addicted to electronics. According to numerous studies, those between the ages of twelve and twenty-two spend an average of seven hours each day on phones, computers, ipads and ipods! This is covert spiritual warfare: keep people preoccupied so they remain incapable of prayer or even thinking of God! The remedy? Living lives based on the Ten Commandments, frequent Mass attendance and ongoing reception of the Sacraments. The God that created the universe can fix anything but it is up to us, His beloved children, to ask for His help in the building of our houses and marriages. Begin a continuous dialogue with Jesus throughout the day: "Lord, what do you think I should do about this? These are some ideas I've had about work, what do you think?" Keep Him in the loop of your life, give Him time and credit. God is alive and He is crazy in love with us! He cares so much that He died for us ... talk to Him! Always remember the importance of constant and consistent prayer, including a daily rosary. Prayer leads to grace. Graces are those amazing gifts that surround us. Many call God's graces "luck." They are too blind to see His love working in their lives because they ignore Him. God is always present to us ... we are the ones who are not present to Him. He does not need us; we need Him more than the air we breathe. God is love and even though we may ignore Him, He continues to love us.

> **We owe God our time and attention.**
> **We owe God our obedient love.**

Share this with your spouse and live your *legacy of love*. Always keep in mind who is building and guarding your house. You are one of God's precious children, baptized into His very life and family. He is your beloved Father. As married Catholics bound together by God's faithful love, analyze how much time is spent with Him versus love for distractions and the strange gods of electronics. How much time is given to God in prayer? What activities or distractions can be removed so that you can increase prayer life? Are you setting time aside to pray the rosary, a chaplet or to make even a quick visit before the Blessed Sacrament? Distractions will never bring the peace and joy that a closer relationship with God and spouse will bring. Your spouse and children spell love T-I-M-E. God spells it that way too! Build your house and protect your family with obedient love and devotion of God.

Perfect Love

"For if you love those who love you, what reward have you?
Do not even the tax collectors do the same? And if you salute only
your breathren, what more are you doing than others? Do not even
the Gentiles do the same? You, therefore, must be perfect,
as your heavenly Father is perfect" (Mt 5:46-48).

We are to follow Jesus who said love your enemies and pray for your persecutors. Hopefully, we do not view our beloved spouse as an enemy or persecutor but the person we fell in love with and want to spend the rest of our life with. We are no better than the hated tax collector if we allow Satan to destroy our love by dredging up painful words and actions of the past or present. We must be aware of his presence and desire to destroy our marriage, work on emptying our heart of pain and daily make the decision to love.

"Put on then, as God's chosen ones, holy and beloved, compassion, kindness, lowliness, meekness, and patience, forbearing one another and, if one has a complaint against another, forgiving each other; as the Lord has forgiven you, so you also must forgive. And over all these put on love, which binds everything together in perfect harmony" (Col 3:12-14). St. Paul is spelling out how we are to be perfected in love like our Father in heaven. Of course, it would be great if our spouse was loving and lovable but if they are not, we need to be patient. Perfection is a change toward holiness that Satan will fight. Change

17

takes time and diligence. It can lead to frustration when it does not work right away. But, continual love and sacramental grace is like water on hard stone; it breaks down the hard heart and makes way for love to be renewed.

We are to be compassionate and kind in living our vows of love and honor for our spouse. We are to willingly initiate necessary changes in our marriage because of the recognition that we are a Sacrament and made in the divine image. We serve and sacrifice without complaining and forgive when our spouse has offended us. This is the love that binds all together in perfection. Do these words seem impossible to live out? They will be without the graces Jesus provides in the Sacraments. Those who are willing to love at a deeper level, engage in ongoing couple prayer and open to cooperating with the graces Jesus bestows in the Sacraments may achieve this level of love sooner than predicted . . . because nothing is impossible with God.

God is perfect love. He sent His Son to teach us how to love perfectly. Jesus loved His Father perfectly by obediently dying on the cross. His call to perfection is a call to begin the journey for personal holiness based on a disciplined obedience to the will of God. This is based on self-control and sacrificial love rather than holding onto hurt to punish our spouse and attempt to control those around us with our will.

As married sacramental spouses, we too are called to do what is hard a hundred times a day as we live our love for God and spouse. When we live sacrificial love like Jesus, there will be suffering as we choose to obediently die on the cross of our self-centered, selfish behaviors. Look at a crucifix and try to relate to the outrageous agony God's Son suffered for us sinners. Jesus allowed a crown of thorns to be jammed into His head. He did not throw down the cross or as the first nail was pounded into His hand say, "That's enough." He accepted all of it to the bitter end, teaching us to stay the course through perfect love.

During the very difficult times of our lives, especially when our spouse and marriage are causing great pain, we are to live our love for Jesus and our spouse in humble obedience. We too are called on to say, "Not my will, Father, but Yours." Staying the course and loving when it is difficult is what we must do; our Sacrament is to be greater than hurt feelings and pride. Being fully human, Jesus knew firsthand the difficulties of life and the taunting traps of Satan. That is why He gave His Church the Sacraments. When received with an open heart, they become grace-filled opportunities for personal perfection and holiness. They help strengthen us in our struggle with obedient suffering, especially in our most difficult times; they are a means to perfection.

In a sacramental marriage, we are one with our spouse and are responsible to encourage and help our beloved to heaven by the words we speak and the actions we take. When only one spouse is praying and receiving the Sacraments, they must persevere in perfect love to bring their spouse into a better relationship with Jesus. Carrying a cross is a humble and humiliating experience. Jesus received help carrying His cross and He will help us carry ours during the difficult times of our marriage. His assistance comes from prayer, the Sacraments and forgiveness. Our sincere, genuine desire to forgive will be a clear message that we want to be perfected like Him who forgives us our sins in the most magnanimous way. Difficult marriages teach us to love when we feel our spouse does not deserve our love. It is then Jesus is perfecting our love by asking us to love, serve, sacrifice and forgive with His grace.

We have worked with many couples whose situation is truly desperate. Their spouse is dealing with serious sin, perhaps even betraying their love and marital vows. Their family and friends suggest divorce. We ask, "How do you feel about this betrayal?" They cry and say, "I'm hurt, humiliated, alone, angry, bitter" and speak of wanting to get even. We ask, "If your spouse was blind and needed assistance, would you obtain a service dog and assist in their learning braille?" They answer: "Yes, of course." We ask, "If your spouse became physically ill, would you be with them through the procedures and treatments?" Again, they answer: "Yes, of course." We ask them to remain one in their Sacrament despite their present hurt and anger, knowing their spouse has become spiritually blind and ill. We stress the Sacrament of Reconciliation where they can ask Jesus for the graces for a clean heart to remove their hurt and anger and to constantly pray for their spouse to be healed and return to God and their marriage.

Sin is contagious. Satan uses the sin of one spouse to infect the other. He allows the sin of one person to negatively affect and hurt another: the victim now experiences the sin of refusing to forgive, contracting anger and revenge in their once clean heart. Satan is like a very contagious disease whose hooks run deep but he will eventually be rendered ineffective when confronted with Jesus' powerful, divine, sacramental grace. This does not work immediately . . . but it does work! Be persistent!

The decision to love can be hard and painful in a difficult marriage. Holy, sacrificial love conquers all. Sacramental marriage is holy. Jesus has shown us how to be perfected in love. We must pray without ceasing for His perfect love to increase our capacity to love sacrificially, with service, honor, respect and forgiveness for our beloved. In a Catholic marriage, we hold nothing back: it is forgiving, faithful, life giving, fruitful and permanent, as is Christ's love for His Church. Catholic marriage is to mirror Christ's perfect love for His Bride, the Church for whom He died.

Share this with your spouse and live your *legacy of love*. In the Sacrament of Reconciliation, ask Jesus for the grace and strength to be perfected. Begin to treat your difficult spouse with tender compassion. Remember, forgive and you will be forgiven. Acting out is a sign of the pain they are carrying. The Divine Physician is calling you both to the Sacrament of Reconciliation to heal your lives, souls and marriage. You have an obligation to address behaviors that are sinful or hurtful but must do so in a loving, kind way. Are you helping your beloved spouse achieve holiness? If they are closed and react negatively toward your concern for them by refusing the Sacrament of Reconciliation, it remains your job, as their beloved, to pray when they are in darkness and blinded by sin just as you would want their help through the darkness of your sin. Be patient. This is the path to sanctification; it is the cross you bear out of love, just as Jesus bore the cross of your sins out of love for you. His cross was far heavier than yours. He forgave His executioners; you must forgive your spouse's sins.

Sanctification

"So if there is any encouragement in Christ, any incentive of love, any participation in the Spirit, any affection and sympathy, complete my joy by being of the same mind, having the same love, being in full accord and of one mind. Do nothing out of selfishness or conceit, but in humility count others better than yourselves. Let each of you look not only to his own interests, but also to the interests of others. Have this mind among yourselves, which was in Christ Jesus, who, though He was in the form of God, did not count equality with God a thing to be grasped, but emptied Himself, taking on the form of a servant, being born in the likeness of men. And being found in human form He humbled Himself and became obedient unto death, even death on a cross" (Phil 2:1-8).

"Therefore, my beloved, as you have always obeyed, so now, not only as in my presence but much more in my absence, work out your own salvation with fear and trembling; For God is at work in you, both to will and to work for his good pleasure" (Phil 2:12-13).

"Working out our salvation" is choosing to be obedient when we do not care to. Marriage is a real test of obedient love for both God and spouse. Jesus provides us with the gifts of sacramen-

21

tal grace to help us be of the same mind, having the same love and being in full accord with our spouse. We are to remove self-ishness and conceit and become humble in all things, working toward sacrificial love. The ideal is both spouses obediently living their love by placing spouse ahead of self. Yes, that is the ideal. The reality, however, is that there is pain in marriage and often rooted in a spiritual battle. When one spouse becomes the source of sin and pain, the offended spouse must realize they are in a spiritual battle for their spouse's soul. Satan seeks to provoke the offended spouse to return hurt for hurt and pain for pain, together with arguments and angry words to be hurled back and forth. Instead, attend the Sacrament of Reconciliation to let go of the hurt and pain; receive the strength and graces Jesus can give to heal broken hearts.

"And do not grieve the Holy Spirit of God, in whom you were sealed for the day of redemption. Let all bitterness and wrath and anger and clamor and slander be put away from you, with all malice, and be kind to one another, tenderhearted, forgiving one another, as God in Christ forgave you" (Eph 4:30-32). The Holy Spirit wants to encourage us to be sanctified in love and truth. Replacing bitterness and anger with kindness and forgiving each other is a holy witness of love. A tenderhearted person is one who is sensitive to words or actions taken against another and how they may feel if slighted, spoken to or acted toward in an unkind, unloving manner. A tenderhearted person is not proud, thinking first of themselves but thinking first and always of others.

> **Love is obedience.**
> **Obedience is love.**

Jesus desires us to live holy lives of obedience and be witnesses to the world. *"You are the light of the world. Let your light so shine before men, that they may see your good works and give glory to your Father who is in heaven"* (Mt 5:14a, 16). Obedience glorifies the Father; therefore, we are not to let the culture influence us. The light we shine on our culture is the obedient light of Jesus who provides us with sacramental graces to help grow in holiness. We receive the divine life of Jesus in each Sacrament, opening us more and more to His love and mercy, enabling us to cooperate with the graces we need as He molds us into new beings, working out our salvation in fear and trembling.

If only the one billion Catholics in the world could realize the power of the Sacraments, understanding they contain the divine life of Jesus. In the Sacrament of Baptism, original sin is washed away as we are baptized into Christ, becoming a child of God. In the Sacrament of Reconciliation, we are forgiven personal sins and given the necessary graces and strength to avoid further sin. In the Sacrament of the Eucharist, we are given the actual body, blood, soul and divinity of Jesus in a transfusion of divine grace. We contain the very life of Jesus when we receive Him and cooperate with His graces to strengthen our resolve against sin. In Catholic marriage, husband and wife become the Sacrament. Unfortunately, when couples refuse to live their married state as a Sacrament, they give scandal to others. Catholics are shocked to hear of Sacraments being desecrated. Yet, Catholic couples desecrate their sacramental marriage and vows by mistreating each other and not living their love and honor for their spouse, given to them as a gift from God.

St. Paul tells us, *"I appeal to you therefore, brethren, by the mercies of God, to present your bodies as a living sacrifice, holy and acceptable to God, which is your spiritual worship. Do not be conformed to this world but be transformed by the renewal of your mind, that you may prove what is the will of God, what is good and acceptable and perfect"* (Rom 12:1-2). It is Jesus living through us that is good, acceptable and perfect. It is He in the Sacraments that provides the necessary graces for our transformation. We, as Catholics, are to be conformed to Jesus and not the culture.

Suffering also transforms us and can lead to our sanctification. Jesus' crucifixion was a mighty work, offering salvation to those who would believe and accept it. Jesus, in turn, allows us as His followers to offer our suffering with Him on the cross as redemptive suffering for our spouse, family and marriage. We do not suffer in vain if we offer our suffering with and to Jesus. Jesus did not quit the cross and we must not quit our spouse or our marriage.

Share this with your spouse and live your *legacy of love*. Still arguing over the same unresolved issues time and time again? Do each of you insist your spouse needs to change first? Do each of you refuse to initiate a change in your behavior? Break this cycle. Your marriage is more important than your pride. Tell your spouse you are going to love them as Jesus desires and become an initiator of change. You be the one to change first. Lead change in your marriage. Choose one behavior your spouse has asked you to work on, just one "little thing" and do it with joy. Think of one thing you can do to grow closer to God and one thing you can do to grow closer to your beloved spouse. This week put into practice one new idea to grow in love and obedience to God.

Our Second Priority:

To Live Our Love for Our Spouse

II

Our Second Priority:
To Live Our Love for Our Spouse

"And the second is like it, love your neighbor as yourself"
(Mt 22:39).
"Be subject to one another out of reverence for Christ"
(Eph 5:25).

Our sacramental spouse is a precious gift from God . . . and our first neighbor! We are to love and cherish them because of the sacred oath we took on our wedding day and because it is how we are to live our love and reverence for Christ.

Romance is easy. Love is hard. The most beautiful and authentic act of love the world has ever known was Jesus laying His life down for His Bride, the Church. True love in a Catholic marriage is lived when both spouses willingly die to their own personal selfishness by placing their spouse's needs before their own. Love then becomes self-sacrificing and self-donating for the good of one's beloved, their sacramental marriage and their children. It is the responsibility of husbands and wives to help each other grow in goodness and holy love for God and each other.

St. James tells us, *"For as the body apart from the spirit is dead, so faith apart from works is dead"* (Ja 2:26). Our faith in God is lived by our works of obedient love for God and our sacrificial love for our spouse. Each of us has been given a mission field to "work" just as the Apostles and Saints. As married Catholics, our mission field and our work is to live our love for our spouse and family. Sounds easy, right? No, it is not! Real love requires self-sacrifice, service and serious personal change. It requires loving our spouse rather than our own selfishness or stubbornly insisting on our own way. Mission fields require obedient love, prayer, selflessness and sacramental grace to stay the course. Jesus served everyone who came to Him with a loving, gracious heart. Scripture frequently says He was moved with pity for the lost, sinful and hurting.

With humble obedience, we are to do the will of God, picking up our cross and carrying it with love... daily. Just like the Apostles and Saints, we are to live in humble, loving, sacrificial service to God, guiding our family to holiness, bringing each member closer to Jesus by our works of self-donation. In doing so, we will teach the next generation how to live their love. Loving and honoring in good times and bad, in sickness and health can be incredibly difficult. We cannot do this on our own but are to humbly and obediently follow God's will, completely dependent on the graces given to us by Jesus in the Sacraments. Through His grace we will attain our sanctification.

Successful mission fields come from gracious hearts who want to serve. They are built on joyful giving, humility and appreciation. Givers are gracious and desire to help. They love the nine little miracle words that initiate sharing and giving: "What do you need and how can I help?" The problem or burden is then shared and their spouse does not feel alone. A generous heart gives time and attention. Love is an action word and is spelled "T-I-M-E." Be present to your spouse and ready to help. And remember, God loves a joyful giver with a gracious heart. Do the words "joyful giver" and "gracious heart" describe you? Is there gratitude in your heart, thankful to God for your spouse and family? Are you thankful for both the good and not so good that happens in your life, understanding God has a plan even though you may not agree with it? Do you lovingly give, knowing what is needed and not count the cost? Are you aware that living your love is paying attention, listening and giving what is needed? Recall St. Paul's words, *"Remembering the words of the Lord Jesus, how he said, 'It is more blessed to give than to receive'"* (Acts 20:35b).

Become aware of all your spouse does and affirm their words and actions. "Thank you for all you do," "I love you," "I am sorry" and "I am so glad I married you" are words of genuine affirmation and can bring peace and a happier home.

Share this with your spouse and live your *legacy of love*. If you struggle with graciousness and giving, attend the Sacrament of Reconciliation. Ask Jesus for the strength and grace to be more loving, generous, self-sacrificing and selfless. It may take several visits but if you are determined, you can also become a gracious giver. Begin today to become appreciative in words and actions for the gift of your beloved spouse. Let them know they are a gift; call them "beloved." Many spouses desire a kind word and encouragement that rarely comes. It is too easy to presume your spouse knows you love and appreciate them and all they do for you and your family. Be the role model of love and appreciation. Givers pray and give love, kindness, appreciation and service constantly. Be a giver.

And remember the nine miracle words: "What do you need and how can I help?"

Our Covenant

"Therefore a man leaves his father and his mother and clings to his wife, and they become one flesh" (Gen 2:24).

This quote is so important that it is repeated in St. Matthew's Gospel (Mt 19:5), St. Mark's Gospel (Mk 10:7) and in St. Paul's letter to the Ephesians (Eph 5:31). These scriptural passages set the essential framework for a marriage covenant between God, husband and wife. A covenant is so much more than a mere contract as it cannot be broken. God is ever involved, an active participant in the relationship of a Catholic husband and wife. When God speaks, we need to listen. When His message is repeated three additional times in the New Testament, we must really listen and pay attention: something very important is being said!

"For the wife does not rule over her own body, but the husband does; likewise the husband does not rule over his own body, but the wife does" (1Cor 7:4). Our marital covenant is about the free giving and accepting that takes place in a Catholic, sacramental marriage, including the giving and accepting of bodies which forever unifies the unbroken bond between God, husband and wife. This is in direct opposition to the thinking of our secular culture that even in marriage, "What's mine is mine . . . my body is mine; what's your is yours . . . your body is yours . . . there is no ours." What crazy thinking!

It is important for couples preparing for marriage as well as those who are already married to understand the significance and seriousness of Catholic marriage as a Sacrament, a Sacred Oath, a covenant and lifelong vocation. Catholic marriage is not based on fun; it is serious business. People prepare for many years to enter a chosen career, sometimes change careers and eventually retire. However, there is no retiring from Catholic marriage, no backdoor. It is important to be well-prepared for the lifelong, binding commitment that lies ahead.

Marriage was designed by God and elevated to a Sacrament by Jesus at Cana. It profits men, women and society. Marriage is a time of great growth for each spouse as they now must think first of their beloved, growing together as one, without outside interference and without thinking they are a separate person and can do as they please. They learn it is no longer "my" way but "our" way. When both spouses live their love for each other, giving of themselves 100% of the time, their marriage will be joyful because it will be God centered. However, when couples make decisions corrupted by selfishness that work against their covenant or engage in personal sin, their marriage will be very difficult and painful.

Sacramental wedding vows are rooted in the wisdom of the Catholic Church and are very serious: "I will love and honor you in good times and bad, in sickness and health until death." The couple is to understand they are entering into a covenant with God and that their union is a permanent, holy exchange that cannot be broken. Their sacramental marriage is binding, exclusive, indissoluble, faithful and mutually self-giving. God does not renege once He has entered a covenant. Civil contracts are an exchange of goods and commodities. However, a Catholic marriage is so much more: God enters the couple's relationship sacramentally, always present, providing them with His graces to weather the storms and carry the crosses they will encounter through the years. Catholic couples do not write their own vows because many of them are too shortsighted to understand the scope of their lives and all that may be required from them in the name of holy, self-sacrificing love. Catholic marriage vows are very serious, far reaching and apply to all life experiences. Contrast this with a non-Catholic or civil marriage where couples marry in a variety of outdoor venues or hotels, writing cute vows such as, "I will love you until butterflies cease to fly" or "I will always love your cute smile." When the hard times begin, some couples may want to bolt saying, "I didn't sign up for this." However, the Catholic couple understands what they signed up for: to love and honor through the bad and sick times as well as the good and healthy times.

Catholic marriage is to follow in the footsteps of Christ who died for His Bride, the Church. In the agony of His crucifixion, He did not come down from the cross because it was "too hard." He finished His mission by dying for His Bride so she could live. When we die to our hurt feelings and self-centered thinking, we breathe new life and love into our marriage, changing our selfish behaviors for our sacramental spouse. This powerful virtue requires a great deal of sacramental grace to achieve, dying to ourselves for our beloved! But there is more: we are also to forgive our spouse

31

when they sin against us and their vows. Jesus promised us a cross and there will be times when couples will easily fall into the "sick of heart" and "bad times" phases of marriage. They may have long forgotten the beauty of their wedding day and now feel their vows are a sham because of the intolerable conditions of hurt and discouragement. Their marriage may be at the breaking point, communication filled with anger and resentment. They are often antagonistic, refusing to cooperate, listen or understand. They are impatient and scoff at any effort of forgiveness. What they fail to realize is that they are each feeling the very same emotions, both engulfed in pain, hurt and betrayal of vows, holding onto toxic words and actions. They each want the other to change, be sorry and apologize. She cries and he raises his voice! She accuses and he rolls his eyes! He swears and she rolls her eyes! They feel they are right and know their spouse is wrong. They wonder if they have made a huge mistake. STOP! This is Satan talking, coaxing us all to give up and quit. Instead, run to adoration or pick up a rosary and pray for Blessed Mother to intercede with the needed graces to be strong and endure the bad times. Remember, every marriage faces "bad times" as God works on hard hearts, trying to soften them to love. Part of this is to bring the couple closer to the oneness of the marriage covenant whereby they depend on Jesus for His wisdom, grace and spiritual help as they cling to each other.

When hanging from the cross, beaten to a pulp, Jesus asked His Father to forgive His executioners. That is the model He gave us to forgive our spouse. If this seems impossible, you are right! It is completely impossible with our puny, human hearts. But, you are not alone in your marriage. Jesus is truly present. Catholic couples must keep Jesus in their lives through individual and couple prayer. Are you praying, individually and as a couple? Are you receiving the Sacraments, especially the Sacrament of Reconciliation? If you answered "yes" then you are receiving the promise of His continual graces to live and love as He has asked. Jesus and His sacramental graces fill in the gaps and shortcomings of our incomplete capacity to love with His all-powerful, unending, complete capacity to love and forgive.

Understand, the "bad" and "sick" times are phases. Life is a journey and marriage is part of that journey, filled with ups and downs. Yes, the ups and downs are more painful than those endured in childhood because this is the time for our souls to grow and become the beautiful, sparkling gems of love that God originally intended in making man in His image and likeness. God is all loving and all forgiving. That is why Catholic marriage vows emphasize how we are to love and honor: in good times and bad until separated by death. Blending individual ideas and personalities will take years of ups and downs but we cannot quit because things become difficult. Can you imagine a person insisting to get off an airplane midflight because of turbulence? We will all have turbulence on our marital journey; we need to ride it out.

The Church knows marriage is hard work and wants every couple to understand all marriages are tested, "*So that the genuineness of your faith, more precious than gold which though perishable is tested by fire, may rebound to praise and glory and honor at the revelation of Jesus Christ*" (1Pt 1:7). Just as golden wedding bands undergo severe heat to remove impurities, so are marriages tested to endure the flame of bad times, including chronic debilitating illness, infertility, miscarriage, addiction, infidelity or loss of income. God's purpose in allowing hardships is to remove the impurity of self-love, teaching sacrificial love and the importance of dying to self for the good of one's beloved. Jesus' presence provides the couple with the needed graces to strengthen their Sacrament through hardships.

Accepting a hardship with patient, loving endurance is not an easy task but in continuing to love and to live The Five Priorities of a holy, Catholic marriage, a husband and wife become the

Gospel lived in "3D" for all who encounter them. St. Francis of Assisi famously said that he preached the Gospel and sometimes he used words. Our lives are the witnesses of true love sacrificed and lived. Jesus is always with those who suffer and who offer their suffering to Him. When we offer our suffering to Him on the cross, it becomes powerful and redemptive; we become united with Him. Our love, lived through hardship, is the witness we give for others to learn what sacramental marriage is and to give glory to God. Living our love for both God and spouse in bad and hard times is proof of Jesus' presence in our Sacrament.

Share this with your spouse and live your *legacy of love*. Hardships sanctify you when offered to the crucified Jesus. Rely on His grace to see you through. Can you begin to accept setbacks as opportunities to submit your will to God as a couple united in love? Can you persevere in prayer to increase your capacity to love God and spouse and always remember holy love endures?

More Than One Flesh

"For this reason a man shall leave his father and mother and be joined to his wife, and the two shall become one" (Mt 19:5).

As mentioned in "Our Covenant," this quote is found four times in Scripture. One would think the focus of the problem would be the new wife and her mother but it is the husband's parents (most often his mother) who have the umbilical cord wrapped tightly around his heart and mind, resulting in the near exclusion of his wife from the marital relationship.

To be clear, this is not about a son's attention and kindness to his mother with respect to the Fourth Commandment. Rather, it is about control of the son by his mother to intentionally belittle, demean and persecute his beloved spouse because she does not follow her mother-in-law's strict wishes, commands and orders. When wives have not followed their mother-in-law's personal game plan, the son is often manipulated to turn against his wife, accusing her of being an unloving, unkind daughter-in-law. Often, the wife is treated as an outcast and unwelcome in the mother's home. Please do not think these situations happen in some faraway time or place. On the contrary, it is descriptive of intelligent, educated couples we have worked with through the years in marriage mentoring—one or both of whom have advanced degrees and have experienced the entire Catholic marriage preparation program. However, within months after their wedding, they report arguments, confrontations and continual marital stress. We discuss this very real, very serious issue in Chapter 5, "In-laws and Outlaws."

God's wisdom and design is always perfect but we insist on fixing it much like trying to improve the wheel. God wants a newly married couple to learn to depend and rely on each other. It is important they respectfully ask family and friends to give them time and space as they learn to form their own interdependence and work together as husband and wife, growing from the idealized, romantic view of perfect love and perfect marriage to a more realistic, self-sacrificing reality. This is achieved by an ongoing commitment to their sacramental marriage, making the decision to love and living that decision through the ups and downs and the highs and lows of life. The result? An interdependent strength and reliability to a lifelong commitment to one's beloved as they begin functioning as ONE.

To understand the depth of what the marriage relationship is meant to be and how it is to be lived in a unique intimacy with God and spouse, we must realize it encompasses the whole being: soul, spirit, will, mind, heart and body. Couples that grow closer in all these areas achieve the true oneness and intimacy God intended for marriage.

SOUL: Accepting and embracing the commitment to the Sacrament of Marriage instituted by Jesus at the wedding feast of Cana and preserved in the Catholic Church. Understanding, upon completion of the vows given in total honesty and free of restraint, the couple leaves the Church bound together as a faithful, fruitful and permanent Sacrament. This is the oneness of the soul: Christ, husband and wife, forever and always sharing, loving and serving.

SPIRIT: Accepting and embracing the commitment to remain one in spirit as each has been baptized in the name of the Father, Son and Holy Spirit. Understanding they both contain the Trinity, who made them in their image and likeness, adopted them at the Sacrament of Baptism, fed them with the body, blood, soul and divinity of Christ, reconciled them, forgave them their sins and sealed them with the graces found in the divine life of Christ. These are two people bound together in the intimacy of God's sacred spirit.

WILL: Accepting and embracing the commitment of a unified free will, making the lifelong choice to love "in good times and bad, in sickness and health." Understanding they will be tested but determined to remain dedicated to God and each other.

MIND: Accepting and embracing the commitment to understand and appreciate each other's thoughts and ideas. Understanding they are to work to find common ground when differing thoughts are expressed, leading to cooperation, compromise and compatibility rather than to control through anger, manipulation or ridicule. The goal is to come together in their ideas, supporting each other, relying on Sacred Scripture and the truth Jesus gave to His Church founded on the Apostles and preserved by the Holy Spirit.

HEART: Accepting and embracing the commitment to be one in heart. Understanding they are to love their spouse so completely they would never hurt them or do anything to break their trust. Their goal is to remain close to the Sacraments, aware of all that can separate them from faithful love, knowing Satan will continue to present the Seven Deadly Sins to destroy their sacramental marriage by presenting enticing thoughts and desires that are not of God.

BODY: Accepting and embracing the commitment to physically love one another. Spouses experience each other's love and devotion through physical intimacy that begins with the emotional sharing of true hearts by listening, understanding, supporting and encouraging each other in their respective roles as spouses and parents. Both husband and wife can trust each other when they confide, share and undress their hearts, knowing their beloved would never hurt them. Each freely gives themselves physically to their beloved as they are each living their love for the other by dying to selfishness. This is true intimacy: two becoming one flesh.

God designed the heavens, the earth and the entire universe. Ask any scientist: it is a brilliant design, a perfect habitat for life to grow and for God's ultimately designed creature to prosper. Mankind is God's masterpiece, gifted with His divine image and He desires an intimate relationship with him. He allows mankind to be fruitful in a manner entirely different from animals who procreate merely by instinct. Husband and wife come together in intimacy with a vow and a decision to love that reflects the beauty of God's love: fruitful, sacrificial and holy. This culminates in the desire to bring one's spouse closer to the purity of God's love, always selfless, never lustful. Lust is using another for one's own selfish gratification. There is nothing holy about lust.

God's plan is perfect. His design for each man and woman becoming husband and wife has the purpose of unitive, selfless love and procreation. God used both form and function in His purposeful design of a man and woman's physical and emotional makeup. The form makes the function work for the intended purpose. God designed the man and woman's body to fit together for both procreation and pleasure but they are to fit together more than just physically.

They are to:
1. Complete each other by filling in where each is lacking or requires assistance.
2. Balance each other physically and emotionally.
3. Respect each other's unique differences.
4. Work together to be compatible, not combative.

The woman's unique physical and emotional makeup is intuitive, sensitive and feminine along with the tough internal endurance and resilience brought about by ever-changing monthly cycles and childbirth. In contrast, men are endowed with physical strength to protect their family as well as passion, ambition and the desire to provide. Both desire their love to be fruitful and creative. They live their love for their children by first living their obedient love for God and then for each other through attention and service. As a couple united in their love for God and each other, they provide a loving, safe home for the protection of their children, teaching them to go forth into the world pleasing God and creating their own families.

The Designer and His design.
The Author and His unique authority.

God's perfect plan is based on love, obedience, sacrifice and holiness. Satan operates in hate, disobedience, selfishness and destruction; holiness is not a word in his vocabulary. Instead, Satan emphasizes self-centered fun, physical pleasure and freedom to do what we want, when we want and with whom we want. He is constantly at work, attempting to keep us off balance and distracted. Married life is hard work. We fall in love, have a beautiful wedding, beautiful children but soon experience the huge burdens of responsibility to care for each other and family. The result is often a lack of proper rest and sleep, little or no time to connect and communicate, frustration, anger, financial stress and constant assaults from our godless culture. Catholics must understand their marriage is countercultural and must always rely on Jesus, ever present in their Sacrament. If we stay connected to the Sacraments, personal prayer, couple prayer, Scripture, service and obedience to the Father's will, with God's great grace, we will live a marriage of sanctification. Do not let Satan win. Know the road will be fraught with exhaustion, setbacks, frustration and discouragement. Achieving holiness in marriage is hard work! But, God never asks for the impossible . . . as nothing is impossible with God.

Share this with your spouse and live your *legacy of love*. Remaining close to the Sacraments will bring you into a deeper intimacy with your spouse and help you grow in love as you work to put aside selfishness and become one in soul, spirit, will, mind, heart and body. Baptized into Christ's body, the Church, you are to remain submissive to Him and His teachings. As Catholic spouses, you are also to remain on the same mission to glorify the Father and one day return to Him. Rededicate yourselves and your marriage to Jesus. He is the perfect part of your Sacrament, the source of joy, peace and faithful love. Live The Five Priorities of a healthy, happy, holy, sacramental marriage and remember disordered priorities cause chaos. It is critical to keep personal prayer life and couple prayer life alive, loving God and serving each other. Everyday ask what you can do as real, concrete evidence of your love for God and spouse.

This is Catholic marriage!

Are You a Model?

"Then the man said, this at last, is bone of my bones and flesh of my flesh; she shall be called Woman, because she was taken out of Man"
(Gen 2:23).

Sounds like a perfect plan, right? Adam took one look at Eve and could not contain his joy. Here was another whose body was compatible and complimentary with his; they were designed to complete each other. God's original plan for this couple to live in peace and harmony was off to a great start. However, this wonderful plan went off track almost immediately. In Chapter Three of Genesis, Adam speaks with blaming disgust to God about this precious gift of a wife, telling Him that the woman He gave him was at fault because she gave him the forbidden fruit to eat . . . conveniently forgetting he too possessed the gift of free will! As we know, they both realized their disobedience and attempted to hide from their sin and God. When God approached, neither apologized: Adam blamed God for giving him Eve, while Eve blamed the serpent. In one chapter, our first parents were tempted by Satan, became convinced their loving Father was not trustworthy, disobeyed Him, sinned, refused to take personal responsibility and did not apologize. How many of us fall into the same pattern when we sin? Do we let Satan beguile us into mistrusting God? Disobey God's Commandments? Refuse to take personal responsibility for our sins against God and neighbor? Refuse to apologize through the Sacrament of Reconciliation?

Before God sent Adam and Eve from the Garden, He told them how hard their lives would be because of their disobedience. God told Adam he would toil in the fields and work his entire life. He told Eve she would endure the pain of childbirth and be "subject" to her husband. We do not know how their marriage and lives were after the expulsion. However, we can surmise it was probably brutal, dealing with a very harsh, inhospitable world coupled with the immense pain of remorse, resulting in a very deep sense of loss and regret. We only know a little of their first two sons. Unfortunately, another story ending in disaster! We can presume marriage and family life was anything but loving and peaceful for this family.

Genesis is a teaching tool, composed of many truths from which we can learn. God created everything from nothing. He made mankind in His own image and gave him free will to choose to love. We are the only creatures with these divine gifts. God is love. He is all good, all seeing. He knows when we sin. Our sins injure our relationship with Him and if the sin is deadly, it completely breaks our relationship with Him. However, because of Jesus' great love for us, He gave His Church the Sacrament of Reconciliation. We admit wrongdoing, have sincere sorrow for our sins and begin anew with the priest's words, "I absolve you from your sins." If only our first parents could have been sincerely sorry, apologized, taken personal responsibility and allowed God to be merciful. If they did, Chapter Three of Genesis might have ended on a happier note and future generations spared the pain and sorrow of sin.

Are we following Adam and Eve's model for marriage? It is the model responsible for the 66% divorce rate. Today, so many couples leave God out of their marriage and follow the model based on our fallen nature inherited from our first parents. When couples selfishly sin, they often add several other sins such as lying, blaming and hiding the truth, all of which fracture their relationship even more with God and spouse. Where there was one sin there are now many. It is a terrible and painful way to live.

The Catholic model for marriage is much different, based upon Jesus' dying for His precious Bride, the Church. He dies so She may have life. This is the model of sacrificial love. Both spouses are to die to their selfish behaviors out of love for their beloved. This kind of love and commitment produces an enduring marriage and children who experience true love.

Some couples, although married in the Catholic Church,

decide on a secular lifestyle without a sense of respect for their marriage as a Sacrament. Years later, they find themselves as two independent people sharing a bed and living under the same roof but discouraged, disconnected and refusing to address their mutual unhappiness. These people are stuck in the Third Chapter of Genesis, living with a poor attitude, refusing assistance from God who they abandoned and is now a stranger to them, not taking personal responsibility for their actions and refusing to apologize. For those Catholics who have ruptured their relationship with God, we suggest a return to the loving and merciful arms of Jesus. It is time to step into the New Testament where Jesus presents sacramental grace to change sinful natures.

For those who say they will not apologize or admit wrongdoing to their spouse, picture this: while driving, someone hits your new car and speeds away. You call the police but the person is gone, never getting out, apologizing or sharing insurance information. The person had a "no need to say sorry" mindset, thinking an apology was a sign of weakness or unimportant. They brushed off personal responsibility for their actions. Or, how about this picture: you are driving a little too fast, run a red light and plow into another car. You get out of the car, refuse to take responsibility and instead angrily blame the other person, telling them they are the cause of the crash when clearly you were responsible. The lesson from these scenarios? Realize that sincerely apologizing for a wrongdoing can mitigate further problems. However, refusing to apologize and blaming another will result in two problems instead of one: the original problem and now the stubborn refusal to admit wrongdoing. Do you want one problem or two?

A true story about the joy of reconciliation: A young couple met with us, the wife struggling with guilt. She and her husband were very wealthy. They met, fell in love, moved in together and decided to marry. They lived in a mansion. Their wedding and honeymoon were extravagant. She had two designer wedding gowns. Three months after the wedding she began to have reoc-curring thoughts leading to feelings of guilt and destroying her peace. When she walked down the aisle, she wondered, "What does God see?" Those present were dazzled at her beauty and expensive wedding dress but she could not let go of the thoughts, "What does God see? What does my soul look like to God?" She had several sexual encounters prior to marriage as did her spouse. They had not attended Mass for years. Their entire focus was on the exterior beauty of the day, neglecting the condition of their souls. We asked about reconciliation: both admitted staying away from the confessional, afraid the priest would be angry at them. We asked each of them to make an appointment for the Sacrament of Reconciliation with their priest to share all this with him. They both agreed. A few weeks later they called saying it was one of the most joyful experiences they ever had and were "back on track" as practicing Catholics!

Humility is needed to attend the Sacrament of Reconciliation. How often have we entered with a heavy heart and left filled with joy! When we apologize to God, we receive the joy of a happy heart and clean soul. Sin weighs our poor souls down but when we are reconciled with God, we feel joy and are strengthened to fight future temptation. Asking God to forgive us verbally is very important; that is why we confess our sins to a Catholic priest. Consider the horrible appearance of a soul eaten away with dis-obedient and disgusting sin when all it takes is the decision to stop the sin and a sincere apology to Jesus to be renewed and made whole in sacramental reconciliation. Jesus gave us the means to clean and perfect our souls and yet the hard-hearted and proud refuse to accept the gift of washing their sins away. This is akin to a person refusing to be cured of a terrible and painful illness. Making amends to God heals our sick and diseased soul.

Humility is also needed to make amends to one's spouse, to heal their heart and provide the opportunity to repair emotional damage. Do our children witness love and forgiveness flowing from one parent to the other? Or, do they live in a house filled with dissention, disagreement and a lack of forgiveness? Do our children live in peace witnessing a happy, loving marriage and dream of having a similar kind of marriage when they become adults? Do we live our love for our spouse by desiring togetherness, serving them with love, touching them with tenderness, paying attention when they are speaking, never speaking unkindly to or about them and, most importantly, praying for them? Do our children see their parents living their love for each other? Or, do they hear us yelling, using angry words, saying unkind things to and about our spouse, showing frustration and irritation with much of what they say and do?

God designed married love to be joyful and sacramental marriages to be opportunities to teach us to love as He loves. If your marriage has fallen short of this design, fix it . . . today! If you are currently suffering in your marriage, Satan will bombard you with thoughts of discouragement. When you feel like quitting, remind yourself that you are listening to the wrong voice! Adam and Eve should have run to the Father when they heard temptation. When you hear the destructive voice that is divisive, identify him as a liar and pray the Hail Mary or recite the prayer, "Jesus, I trust in You" as often and as many times as necessary.

Children feel very uncomfortable around bickering and arguing but they thrive in a home of joy and peace. When our daughter was in preschool, we were invited to dinner at the home of one of her classmates. After a few minutes we noticed the parents bickered and contradicted each other constantly. When one spoke the other would shake their head or roll their eyes, telling us through their mannerisms their spouse was ridiculous. We politely left after dessert and as we buckled our daughter into her car seat she said, "Let's not go to the argumentative people's house again. They hurt my tummy."

Share this with your spouse and live your *legacy of love*. Remember, you are a Sacrament of the Catholic Church. Harmful, unloving, unkind, disrespectful words and actions are sins against love. Behaving in such a manner is being unfaithful to your vows to "love and honor" each other. Satan hates God, Jesus, His Church, His Sacraments as well as your marriage and family. He desires your marriage to be unhappy and for you to drive your spouse away. Be strong in your decision to have a healthy, happy, holy marriage built on confessing sins against vows to love and honor. Appreciation and encouragement will help a family grow in peace. Your children are watching how you live your love. God is also watching and will bless your efforts to make your marriage holy. God gave you your spouse to love . . . when you meet Jesus, what will you say when He asks, "Did you love and honor your spouse as you promised you would?"

To Serve or Not to Serve

"Even as the Son of man came not to be served but to serve, and to give his life as a ransom for many" (Mt 20:28).

The Gospel accounts are full of Jesus' works of love and service to those who came to Him. The Son of God gave sight to the blind, healed the sick, raised the dead and fed thousands of people. Yet, He humbly knelt before a tax collector and simple fishermen to wash dirty, smelly feet like a common slave. Jesus was always showing us how to love through genuine, humble service.

Satan said, "I will not serve." When a person refuses to serve, like Satan, they are falling into the deadly sins of sloth and pride. "My time, my projects, my level of exhaustion" are all more important than helping or serving. Self-love always stands in the way of serving. "I want to do what I want to do. I don't want to extend myself for you. I'm too tired and too busy to serve you." This thinking has no place in a sacramental marriage. Love is sacrificial service built on love of God and spouse. Expecting to be served is not the path to holiness.

Some spouses have the mistaken idea that each must give 50% for a healthy marriage. The reality is both must give 100%! They must give their all . . . all the time. Too many times a spouse comes home from work and demands to be served. They falsely presume their work and service are complete, believing their job or profession is the entirety of their service. This is a false concept. After all, the home and children belong to both spouses. The primary breadwinner is very important. Provision for the family is essential and genuine appreciation should always be given for this major role and contribution. However, using the argument, "I work so hard for you. When I come home, I'm done and I demand to be served" is a poor excuse. A single person would still need to work to support themselves. It is doubtful they planned on begging for an income. They would have pursued an education or a trade to be employed, knowing they needed a place to live, transportation, clothes and the necessities of life. Returning home, they would still need to deal with chores, marketing and cooking.

God gave us the prototype of division of labor when He told Eve she would have children and Adam would work. Of course, today with our complicated lifestyles, the division of labor needs to fit the individual needs of the family. It may be that mom stays home to care for the children and dad works to provide for them. However, when dad comes home, he is not off duty; there is still much to be done and he can certainly help. He may have certain "dad" tasks he does every night for mom or the children. Or, he may "fill in" wherever he is needed. Remember the magic words, "What do you need and how can I help?" He may oversee baths, help with homework or assist with bedtime prayers, filling in where needed.

If both parents work outside the home, both will need to share the chores. Spouses are to cooperate and help each other accomplish all that needs attention for the smooth running of a family: errands, school conferences, shopping, marketing, cooking, financial and banking issues, homework, doctor appointments, care of cars, pets, carpools and extracurricular activities. It helps to make a list of all the jobs necessary to run the home. Division of labor is a good tactic when delegating the jobs that are needed to run a family and household smoothly. The spouse with the necessary talent or skill becomes the recipient of the job. Just as in the military, education and corporate life, each job has a correct manner of execution as well as time-sensitive deadlines to be addressed when delegating responsibilities. Taking out the trash means taking it out after dinner or when it is full, not when it is overflowing!

These ideas may seem silly to the person who is flexible and giving but these are serious areas of contention when one spouse refuses to help. In marriage, it is essential to work together to meet each other's needs as well as those of your children. When two people work together, life flows more easily. There is no need for continuous reminding and nagging when both spouses are on board with a pleasant attitude, doing their chores correctly and on time. Get the job done right the first time so everyone has more time for healthy, playful opportunities while teaching your children how husbands and wives work together for the common good. Of course, it is wise for both spouses to be able to know how to fill in if the one becomes ill or overwhelmed by other responsibilities. Remember, home is the school of love. When children see their parents working well together, they will learn how to live their love through service now and in the future when they are married.

> **Cooperate and work together.**

God designed us to be helpmates. Too many times people fall in love with a playmate, seeking continual fun. Finding such a playmate, they think they are in love and spend their time taking trips, watching movies, shopping and hiking. This is love . . . right? No, this is not love, just two people having fun with little or no responsibility. This is one of Satan's tricks: let people spend two or three carefree, fun years together and then marry. Eventually, with the reality of life's responsibilities facing them, their vision of a fun, idyllic life together is shattered. The fun is over, replaced by work, service and sacrifice. It is better to look for a helpmate and plan on fun when the work is done or when a break is needed. Learning to cooperate and work well together are very important ingredients in forming a healthy, happy, holy marriage. Equally important is the refusal to be bossy or controlling but to work together to accomplish the many responsibilities without one spouse constantly insisting on their way. The goal of a married couple working together is not only to work well together but to "zig when the other zags," such as, "I'll do this while you do that . . . I'll trim the bush while you rake the clippings . . . I'll paint the trim while you use the roller . . . I'll wash while you dry." Jobs can be switched according to each spouse's ability and interest. A true helpmate is one that is easy going, happy and willing to fill in the blank spaces.

One additional thought: no one sits and watches television or engages in electronics while their spouse works feverishly on the household tasks and cares for the children. Home and children are both parents' responsibility. Both work side by side to get the work done together so they can go to bed together, talking, praying and cuddling.

Share this with your spouse and live your *legacy of love*. Whenever you need help, communicate your thoughts and feelings to your beloved. Without arguing or using angry words, simply state, "It would be really helpful if you could do this for me when I ask." Then it is your spouse's turn to show their love and cooperation by saying, "Ok, I can do that." Please, do not say, "I can do that only if you do this for me." Giving to get is bartering, not love. Spouses need to be able to kindly ask for and receive the help they need. Remember, Jesus is present in your marriage. He reads hearts, sees and hears everything. What does He see when viewing your marriage? Taking advantage of your spouse is against the concept of love and the vows you made. If you have been spoiled by parents in your family of origin, it is time to become a functioning part of your present family. If you have been a selfish spouse, it is time to attend the Sacrament of Reconciliation and ask Jesus to forgive your slothful behavior.

Ghosts in Our Bedroom

"And he said to them, You have a fine way of rejecting the commandment of God, in order to keep your tradition!" (Mk 7:9).

"For out of the heart come evil thoughts, murder, adultery, fornication, theft, false witness, slander. These are what defile a man"
(Mt 15:19, 20a).

Our secular culture rejects the centuries of Judeo-Christian belief that fornication is a sin, that physical intimacy is to be saved for marriage and shared for the first time on the couple's wedding night. The rejection of this most important model has wrought havoc on women, children and families. The secular culture continues to indoctrinate with the dangerous lie that living together is important for a couple to explore their true feelings, save financially and determine whether their relationship merits ongoing commitment. Couples are shocked to learn that the "culturally acceptable" sin of fornication is condemned in Scripture along with murder and stealing (Mt 15:19-20), (Mk 7:21-23), (1Cor 6:13, 18), (Gal 5:19-21) and (1Thes 4:3-8). They are surprised to hear that the seriousness of this sin offends God and destroys their soul and that of their partner. Why is fornication such a serious sin? Because it is the unlawful taking of a privilege given for the first time on one's wedding night, after the vows of lasting love and honor have been exchanged before God, family and friends in a Catholic church. A person's first sexual experience imprints them and can bind them forever to that person in their memory. When a person has devalued their body by giving it to another, they have been one with someone who really was not worthy of this precious gift. They have thrown away the importance of the total giving and receiving of their body for the first time. This is more than a physical giving. It is a giving of complete intimacy involving the entire person physically, mentally and spiritually.

Catholic marriage is a holy vocation and covenant made with a sacred oath. Spouses are to help each other grow closer to God as they live their love for Him and each other in their sacramental marriage. Their goal is to love each other to heaven by doing God's holy will. Sex before marriage is not God's holy will nor is it willing what is best for another, taking them away from God. Women are put at risk because of their ability to conceive. There was a time when men would not put them in such a compromising position. However, today women are at risk, often believing the cunning lie that they are "loved" and fail to grasp the difference between love and lust. A woman's body has become a usable and dispensable item for free sex without contract or commitment. Remember the wolves in sheep's clothing Jesus warned us about? Lambs need protection from those wolves!

Commodities of value require contracts: we cannot purchase a house, car or phone without one. Yet, women are supposed to give their body away for nothing, putting their lives and their future children's lives in clear and present danger? Really? What kind of a fiendish culture would suggest such a thing? Our culture has promoted this kind of behavior in girls as young as ten.

Satan can use memories of previous sexual relationships to weaken and destroy a sacramental union. Either or both spouses may recall memories of previous relationships, assaulting the holiness of their sacramental marriage bed with guilty or tantalizing thoughts from the past. It is one of many attempts Satan uses to negatively impact the Sacrament of Marriage. If thoughts of previous relationships come to mind particularly when you are intimate with your spouse, make it a priority to attend the Sacrament of Reconciliation not just once but every time this happens. Satan will whisper, "It's okay to remember . . . no need to be sorry . . . you aren't doing anything wrong . . . those were wonderful, passionate times to remember." Do not believe him! Do not allow ghosts in the bedroom!

God's laws are laws of love. He created us and He knows us better than we know ourselves. He knows pre-marital sex impacts marriage in a host of unhealthy ways. There can easily be good or bad comparisons or the temptation of grading and judging one's spouse against others. During the difficult times when there is discord, thoughts may wander to a previous sexual relationship, causing a loss of focus on one's spouse or wondering if life would have been happier or easier with a previous lover. Aware of previous relationships, a spouse may become anxious their beloved is remembering, judging or comparing. Both will then suffer from the disobedience of the past.

There are also those situations where one is reminded of a lover who abused trust and caused emotional or physical injury, perhaps even rape. Such relationships can create enormous trust issues as well as unwarranted suspicions of their ever-faithful spouse. Or, there may have been a secret, terminated pregnancy resulting in lifelong feelings of abandonment by their partner, guilt, regret, recrimination, anxiety and depression. Finally, there is the possibility of contracting a sexually transmitted disease that may remain a constant reminder of poor decision making.

We have all heard about the protection of fragile ecosystems. Government agencies preserve various species from outside influences that can negatively impact the ecosystem. The American way of life was a cultural ecosystem that was healthy and worked well with intact, stable families. Women and children generally felt safe because they were respected and protected. People believed in the Judeo-Christian God; obeying His Ten Commandments was a way of life. It was a safer, kinder time. Front doors were unlocked even in metropolitan cities; when everyone is obeying the Ten Commandments, crime and violence are rare. Our cultural ecosystem was successful until the 1960's when social architects began to change the norms and attitudes, initially through the media. As a culture, we became indoctrinated with the new concept that women now had the right to be sexually liberated due to the new wonder drug, the birth control pill. This led to sex on demand as a right by men who no longer felt the need to be married to have sex. Now, they had license to expect sex from a woman anytime without financial or personal responsibility of marriage or children. This supposed "right" was far more beneficial to men than women.

Acting against God has brought devastation to man. God's rules of love are always for mankind's protection . . . not God's. Eve was duped into believing she could eat the forbidden fruit and no harm would be done. Several thousand years later her daughters were also seductively duped into believing they had the right to sexual freedom and in exercising that freedom, no harm would be done. The pill allowed them the right to give their bodies away without love or the protection of the marriage contract. When the pill did not work, the woman was then left alone with an unplanned pregnancy and faced dire options. The fallout to our cultural ecosystem has caused widespread destruction to women and the death of millions of their children. With this new freedom came the destruction of the family: infidelity, divorce, abandonment, abuse, sexually transmitted diseases, rape and abortion. As if this was not destructive enough, Satan further increased this level of human destruction using and abusing the female body through kidnapping and sexual, human trafficking. Only a few generations ago, this would have been unthinkable in any civilized culture. Today, it is a very real fear of parents seeking to protect their precious, innocent daughters who are the holy, Catholic wives and mothers of the future, bringing forth new life made in God's divine image.

When we think we know better than God, the ghosts of our past and present haunt our culture. Who knows us better than God, who made us out of His great love? Obeying God is the only appropriate, healthy option. Adam and Eve listened to Satan and brought evil, sin and death into our world. We too have inherited the weakness of listening to the wrong voice. Satan wants us to believe God's laws of loving protection are unfair, mean and controlling because they do not allow us to do what we want, when we want. If you believe the lie that God is trying to control you through rules of safety and love, reread the previous page. God gifted us free will so we could choose to love Him through our obedience. His rules are not about control but about protection from the effects of evil.

We cannot change the past but we can remain aware of lies of disobedience before we fall prey to Satan's temptations, reminding ourselves how sinful actions can impact our sacramental marriage. All sin can have long-term effects on our mind, body and soul . . . and on our spouse. However, we are blessed to be members of the Church Jesus founded on His Apostles. Knowing mankind's weakness to sin, He gave us the tools to repair the damage we continually do to ourselves and each other through the holy Sacrament of Reconciliation. As Satan presents temptations that lead to deadly sin, we must keep in mind the far-reaching consequences of such sinful choices.

Share this with your spouse and live your *legacy of love*. Every day ask God to increase your capacity to love and be loved; that is His design for your holy marriage. Say the rosary together for peace and purity of heart. If forgiveness of self is difficult, frequent the Sacrament of Reconciliation and recite the Chaplet of Divine Mercy at three in the afternoon every day. This will help mercy flood your soul. The graces from the Sacrament of Reconciliation will heal and strengthen your marriage and the culture.

Marriage Is Hard Work

"I will never fail you nor forsake you" (Heb 13:5b).

"Blessed is the man who endures trial, for when he has stood the test he will receive the crown of life which God has promised to those who love him" (Jas 1:12).

Previous generations struggled through famines, plagues, depressions and world wars. They dealt with these struggles by trusting and depending on God through continuing prayer and reliance on the Sacraments. Our parents and grandparents had one objective: to survive and make a better life for the next generation. We can only imagine the suffering previous generations endured. Suffering still exists but in comparison, our lives are easier. When hardship enters our lives, we ask, "Why me, Lord?" Instead, we should ask, "What are you teaching me, Lord? What do you need me to learn from this?"

Today, little girls are raised on princess stories, expecting a life of romance and fun from Prince Charming. Fantasy programs on television depict gorgeous bachelors and bachelorettes, exotic destinations, fabulous rings, fancy clothes, romantic weddings and palatial parties, seducing a generation into unaffordable and impossible expectations of dream weddings and marriages. Even though these programs are listed as "reality television," they are anything but real as it is all about superficial entertainment, playful encounters and unreal experiences, enticing many to be poisoned by desiring the impossible and unattainable. What young adults see appears wonderful but has no basis for genuine, sacramental married life. Unfortunately, in their minds this is what true love looks like.

On these fantasy programs, the process of weeding through the many hopeful contestants is to decide who will be the most fun and who will love them the best. Their interpretation of love is very self-centered. It is all about "knowing me, knowing how I feel and loving me." The other person's needs and ideas are secondary, because it is all about being the chosen "one." They miss the meaning of love: two people dying to self for their beloved, both giving 100% in good times and bad, in sickness and health. After the decision has been made, the couple appears so happy and takes off into the sunset to begin their perfect, romantic life together. Months later, true reality sets in as the adoring public learns they did not make it. Life with the stresses of true reality have broken their supposed "love."

Authentic love and marriage is hard work because it is selfless, requiring serious, personal change as each spouse daily accommodates to the other. The question is not, "What do I want or need?" Rather, it should be, "What does my spouse want or need?" The true priority is to place our spouse first, serving them, addressing their wants and needs. If each spouse put their beloved before themselves, they would have a healthier marriage. However, this does not happen quickly. It takes time to change self-centered personalities that cause friction in a marriage. Love is a lifelong endeavor; it is fraught with ups and downs. We must always remain vigilant because Satan will do everything to destroy our love and sacramental union. He will always be looking for a way into our imperfect human nature, bringing every deadly sin into our consciousness to take us off track. Satan will cause hurt feelings and outside problems to affect dedication and love. Be ready for these disturbances! Expect them but as followers of Jesus, strive to live a holy, Catholic marriage. It is a great blessing when both spouses are willing to work together, clinging to Jesus and each other through prayer and the Sacraments.

Becoming truly one is more than sex. It is a lifetime process of two people bending out of love for their spouse by growing together in virtue, willing to work on personal change and continually dying to selfish behaviors. This is all part of the oneness of marriage. Is this process easy? No, it is very hard work. Sacramental marriage is not for the weak or lazy! It requires the willingness to shed our self-righteous personalities and to cease believing our way is best. The attitude of "my way or the highway" needs to be replaced with "not my way but God's way for our marriage."

Selfishness is part of our human nature. One spouse willing to grow while the other remains stubborn and unwilling to change is difficult. We must not lose heart or be discouraged! For every action, there is a reaction. As we change, our spouse will also be influenced to change. Changing our behavior will often result in our spouse changing their reactions to us. When a negative comment is made, stop and say with a gentle voice, "That was unkind ... you are better than that." Meet every comment with kindness. Meet anger and unkind behavior with prayer and patience, serving, sacrificing and constantly praying for them. If time permits, attend Mass during the week. Pray the rosary daily for the conversion of their heart. Attend the Sacrament of Reconciliation and share with Jesus the difficulties of marriage. Know that sacramental grace at work in our souls means Jesus is there working with His graces.

A brief story about selfless love: a woman we knew had four children and a very angry, mean-spirited husband. The verbal abuse toward her and the children was unending. As each child became eighteen, they left home to find peace from the barrage of his insults and emotional abuse. Eventually, the last child left and shortly thereafter, so did his wife. She never dissolved the marriage, so it remained a Sacrament. She and her children were able to create new lives free from pain. Years went by and one night there was a knock on her door. Opening it, she saw the fragile shell of the man she once called her husband. Cancer was eating him up and no one would help him. He begged her for help. She took care of him those last months. He died with the priest present, having been forgiven by his family who were by his bedside as he slipped into the arms of Jesus. It was a lesson in love and forgiveness we will never forget.

Share this with your spouse and live your *legacy of love*. Marriage is the only Sacrament involving three people: Jesus, husband and wife. Forgiveness is of great importance in marriage. Every spouse has hurt their beloved. It is important to apologize with all sincerity and attend the Sacrament of Reconciliation to ask for the graces to be a kinder, more loving spouse. Constant prayer and frequent use of this Sacrament will help heal the divisive, unhealthy flaws in your personality. At Mass, allow Jesus to feed you with His divine gift of sacrificial love so mystical, powerful and rich in grace that, with an open heart, you will be infused and transformed into the Christ-like behavior of love and forgiveness.

Our Spouse, Our Cross

"Then Jesus told his disciples, If any man would come after me, let him deny himself and take up his cross and follow me" (Mt 16:24).

If we follow Jesus, we will receive a cross. It is what we do with our cross that brings us either closer to God or further away from Him.

A quick story: Once upon a time, there was a man who told Jesus that his cross was too heavy and he wanted to renegotiate. Jesus led him to a huge room filled with the biggest, thorniest and worst crosses imaginable. The man was horrified at the number of crosses. As he walked through the room, he found in the corner a very small, very smooth, lightweight cross. Jesus smiled and said, "That's that cross I made especially for you, small and smooth so you could carry it." After seeing other people's crosses, the man decided his was just fine.

It is important to remember suffering is transforming, helping us realize we are not in control and must humbly reach out to Jesus for aid. Suffering teaches humility and compassion for others. We come to understand there are many people who are in pain and our worldview becomes less about self and more about others. Whatever the problem, the solution is always prayer and Jesus. He who never sinned accepted His cross so that we who believe and love Him could be given the opportunity for eternal life. Jesus suffered in obeying His Father's holy will and His compassion and mercy for us is beyond our comprehension.

When reading about the lives of the Saints, we see each is given the very difficult job of carrying their own specific cross. Crosses lead to sanctification. They drive us to our knees in desperation as we realize we are not God and that we need Him because we are not in control. It is then we begin to rely on Jesus. This does not mean the cross is removed but we begin to understand that our mission is to pray and submit to Jesus' holy will (not always willingly), finally giving in to Him through love. All of us at some time in our life will be given a cross or many crosses. It may be the death of a loved one, relationship issues, infidelity, financial loss, sickness, mental or emotional issues. We can become angry at God for allowing this to happen or we can accept the cross to the best of our ability, pick it up and carry it with love, knowing it is given by Him for our sanctification and perhaps the sanctification of our spouse and family. When the weight of the cross is too much for us, we run to Jesus in the Sacraments and personal prayer because only Jesus can sustain us.

1. Is our spouse or marriage a cross that we have been asked to carry?

2. Is our spouse difficult?

3. Is our heart broken because of the disconnect from them?

4. Are they disinterested in any kind of change or growth?

5. Are they often unhappy, angry or in a perpetually bad mood?

6. Do they say they will do something and then just not bother?

7. Do they refuse to pray individually or as a couple?

8. Do we sometimes feel we are carrying the whole weight of the world on our shoulders?

Answering "Yes" to any of the above questions means there is work to be done.

Answering "Yes" to any of the above questions does not mean the task is insurmountable.

A true story about a young couple with two small children: the wife was awakened in the middle of the night with a scream for help from her husband. He had awakened to get a drink of water when everything went black. As she rushed toward him, he said, "I'm having a stroke." She dragged him to the bed and called 911, wondering how this could happen to a thirty-four-year-old athlete, healthy and in great physical condition. An artery had broken in his neck and blood flowing through his brain caused about fifty strokes. Their priest came to the hospital to anoint him as four more strokes followed; his wife believed the anointing saved his life. Hours later, his medical team met with his wife and explained how life had now changed. Their prognosis was grim, telling her that her husband would possibly not walk or speak. She nodded without emotion as they spoke. One of the physicians finally said, "Do you understand what we're saying to you?" She said, "Yes I understand but you see I'm Catholic and I took a vow to love and honor in good times and bad and sickness and health until death parted us. I guess this is one of those bad, sick times." The physician replied, "We don't hear that. We usually hear people say that they didn't sign up for this." Two years later, with a great deal of therapy, love, determination and God's grace, he is recovered, has a great job and remains healthy.

The previous story illustrates why Catholic couples do not write their own vows. Individually written vows can be too short-sighted to factor in the many crosses that may enter couples lives. Remember, Jesus knows all about crosses. He had help carrying His and He is standing by to help carry ours . . . if we ask. If we rely on Him and remain close to the Sacraments, He will give us a peace that surpasses all understanding.

> **A quick note:** if someone is in a dangerous marriage, alert law enforcement and have a plan for protection for yourself and your children. Then turn to an understanding priest, a capable Catholic counselor and supportive family members. Prayer and sacrifice can then be offered for the offending spouse in a safe environment.

Share this with your spouse and live your *legacy of love*. You are one with your spouse. It is your responsibility to help each other when the need arises. If your spouse became crippled, you would need to procure a wheelchair and modify the house to accommodate the disability. If your spouse became blind, you would provide the needed training and acquire a guide dog. It follows then when your spouse becomes spiritually crippled or blind, you are to rescue them spiritually! Their problem is most likely based on one of the Seven Deadly Sins; that is why spiritual rescue is needed. Satan sows seeds of discord to destroy marriages, making every family member vulnerable but Jesus is always ready to help carry your cross and break Satan's power. Jesus awaits in the Sacraments to give you strength to preserve in loving service, quiet prayer, fasting and sacrifice. Carrying a cross is never easy; nor is loving someone who is not lovable or loving.

It is hard work! Know Jesus understands abandonment, rejection and crosses.

Free Will

"And he said to them, Follow me, and I will make you fishers of men"
(Mt 4:19).

Although Jesus was speaking to His future Apostles, Peter and Andrew, He asks all of us to follow Him in obedient love for the Father who will direct us in our mission field. With free will, we all have the option to follow or not follow Jesus. We are familiar with the story of the rich young man who approaches Jesus, tells him he has been obedient to the Commandments and wants to know what else he can do to gain eternal life. Jesus invites him to sell all his possessions and follow Him. The young man turns away, too attached to his wealth and material goods. Following Jesus is not always easy. It can be very difficult, the opposite of what we would choose for ourselves. The story of the rich young man is so important for our salvation that it is repeated in the Gospels of St. Matthew (19:16-22), St. Mark (10:17-31) and St. Luke (18:18-30) to emphasize its importance and the necessity of following Jesus by willingly letting go of whatever prevents our sanctification.

All relationships have expectations. God is love and He loves each of us beyond our capacity to understand. If we are to follow Him, we must use our free will to prove our love for Him by choosing to obediently follow His Son. As baptized Catholics, we are expected to know, love and serve God. We follow Jesus to the best of our ability by obeying the Ten Commandments, obeying His teachings handed down to His Church, receiving the Sacraments and confessing our sins when we fall short of our calling to love both God and spouse.

Expectations for our relationship with our spouse are based on our sacramental wedding vows that are sacred oaths and are applicable to all our actions. The ideal expectation and goal of a Catholic, sacramental marriage is based on each spouse living their vows of love and honor under all conditions and circumstances. This is accomplished through willing to freely live one's vows even if their spouse has broken theirs. Unfortunately, we often witness the opposite: couples unwilling to be kind, respectful, serving and forgiving of each other. They refuse to love, honor or respect, continue feeling hurt and react as a child, hurting back. Sometimes the hurt does not even come from their spouse but from a previous experience still being carried like excess baggage. They lash out and refuse to love until they hear, "I'm sorry." However, even after an apology spouses still refuse to forgive because they are incapable of letting go of real or imagined wrongs. They are listening to the "poor me" negative voice of Satan, telling them they have been injured and their spouse does not deserve them, their love or their respect. This self-righteous attitude is the basis of many troubled marriages as the sin of pride rears its ugly head again and again in the oft-repeated mantra of, "I'm right, you're wrong!"

Our relationship with God is one-sided; He gives and we take. God loves each of us even when we do not love Him. He loves the unlovable and the unloving. He loves big sinners, those who say they hate Him and those who say He does not exist. He will do anything to bring a person into a relationship with Him . . . even die on a cross for just one lost lamb. God desires a two-sided relationship with each of us. It is hard to comprehend that the one true, living, loving God, Creator of all, desires a personal relationship with each of us. He calls us frequently throughout the day and our lives. The more we follow, the more our soul reflects Him; it is the house where He lives within us. Because of our free will, we can choose to have a relationship with Him . . . or not. We can choose to love The Great Giver of all gifts . . . or turn our back to

Him. Unfortunately, we too often turn our back to Him, resulting in that one-sided relationship.

God is perfect. He does not need our love but He designed us with free will so we could choose to love Him. Our generous God gave us the gift of free will and we can choose to love Him through an obedient relationship with Him. The word "obedient" makes many of us uncomfortable because we want to do as we please, centering on the concepts: "I will do what I want and when I want," "No one will tell me what to do," "I am free to do as I wish," "I don't like rules; rules are boring." Does this sound like Eve? What were the consequences of her sin? What will be the consequences of our sin when we do what we want when we want? It would be better to answer the call of love from the One who made us, died for us, watches over us and calls us to Him. If we begin to talk to Him in our heart and listen to His voice in the Gospels, we will find something far more satisfying than "our own thing" such as genuine love, direction and peace. Taking our gift of free will for granted would be like a wealthy but miserly person keeping all their money for themselves. We would think, "What a miser, to have all that money and hoard it. What a waste. Look at the good they could be doing. What's wrong with them?"

So, are we "free will" misers? How are we using our free will? Are we using it to love God and our spouse? How are we living our love? Are we choosing to do good or ill, love or hate, give or take? Most important of all, are we freely choosing to obey God or Satan? It is time to tell God we want to love Him. It is only logical to give our gracious and good God our obedient love, not place anything before Him or take His name in vain. Let us attend the Sacrament of Reconciliation and beg His forgiveness. Let us make Mass the centerpiece of our week, being thankful for the sacramental gift of the blessed Eucharist as we receive His body, blood, soul and divinity. Finally, let us consider a continuous dialogue with Him. There is so much to seek His help for such as, "Lord, help me be nice to this person whom I really don't like" or "Lord, give me a kind heart so I can stop belittling my spouse" or "Lord, what should I do about this upcoming problem?"

It is also time for us to utilize our free will to love our spouse the way we vowed and the way they need, deserve and desire to be loved. Our spouse has probably asked us to change or fix many things in our relationship. Just pick one and do it today! Really, no one can force us to love. Marriage is not the military where our commanding officer tells us what to do and we have no choice but to comply. Nor is it the government who says we will pay taxes and follow certain laws with no choice but to comply. Let us be generous and use our free will to choose to know, love and serve God and to choose to know, love and serve our beloved spouse. To accomplish this, we must look to God's greatest gift: His Son, Jesus Christ. It is He who taught us how to love and obey God by living a humble, obedient life of love for His Father and how to love our neighbor through His many examples of serving those who came to Him. It is time we choose to serve our spouse with a generous heart and not the heart of a miser. Seize the opportunity to love. Choose to live obedient love for the Father. Using our free will to love God and obey Him is the purpose of our life. When our lives are off track it is often because we choose not to love.

Secularism teaches:

"Me first, my way."

"I deserve to do as I wish."

"Nobody is going to tell me what to do."

"This is my free time and I'm going to do what I want."

"I made the money and I'll spend it how I please."
"This is who I am. I will not change for you."

Jesus teaches:

Our first neighbor is our beloved spouse.

We are to freely choose to love, honor and respect them

Share this with your spouse and live your *legacy of love*. Be sure your legacy is not a legacy of anger, selfishness or a lack of love and service to God and family. Time is short, so let us turn off the electronics . . . computer, phone, ipad, television . . . and ask your spouse and children, "What do you need and how can I help." Use kind words with everyone, especially one's family. Remember, your words have the power to bring your spouse and family toward you or push them away. Do not be a "free will" miser!

Our Third Priority:

To Live Our Love for Our Children

III

Our Third Priority:
To Live Our Love for Our Children

"And he took a child, and put him in the midst of them; and taking him in his arms, he said to them, Whoever receives one such child in my name receives me; and whoever receives me, receives not me but him who sent me" **(Mk 9:36-37).**

Children are a very special gift from God, a new creation born from fruitful love. God allows us to co-create with Him a new life imprinted with His very image, a gift beyond our comprehension.

Sometimes despite our best efforts as Catholic parents, we fall prey to the lies of our toxic, anti-Catholic culture such as the disproportionate time we believe we must spend on extracurricular activities with our children, completely disrupting family time for communication and prayer. One day, when we meet Jesus at the moment of our death, He will ask, "Do those precious children I sent you know me, love me and serve me by practicing the holy faith I initiated two thousand years ago?" It will be very difficult if we have to reply, "Well, not exactly. We frequently needed to skip Mass and never really had time for family prayer because of sports, dance and other activities but the kids did really well in all those things." What will Jesus say? If we are so focused on extracurricular activities, to the extent that we rarely have time for meals together or skip Mass and family prayer, we will have denied our children the formation of a sincere relationship with Jesus, one that will protect them on their tumultuous journey through life. What is more important to our children's spiritual and moral development than doing what Jesus taught?

If we have not followed this process of spiritual and moral development, it is time to rethink the family schedule of activities based upon The Five Priorities. No parent intentionally places their children's immortal souls at risk but children practice what they live and learn in their families. They will take with them into adulthood what they learned in childhood. This is good news if parents have raised and educated their children in the faith, living and loving Jesus as their number one priority. These children will live their faith-filled life and eventually raise their children with the same Catholic principles. Living a holy marriage and raising holy children was the focus of Catholic marriage until hijacked some sixty years ago by our secular culture, resulting in the breakdown of family and culture. Today, children know many neighborhood and school friends traveling back and forth between their divorced parents sharing custody and hear their friends talk about the ongoing arguing that still takes place. Think divorce is the answer to making life better? Think living in two different homes with two different sets of rules and regulations or even one home with an absence of rules or regulations are good ideas?

Both parents living their love for God first and their spouse second is one of the greatest gifts we can give our children. They will then grow and develop in a healthy, happy, holy marriage, feeling loved, safe and content. They will learn the love of God by living in a home with a kind, loving father who is faithful to his family by serving his wife and children. They will learn the love of family as they watch their mother love and serve their father and siblings with a joyful heart. An ongoing, healthy cycle results: parents who serve their family, die to their own selfishness and remain faithful and dependable, teach their children the self-sacrificing, loving model they will repeat one day when they become parents.

Many couples say their children are their first priority. This actually jeopardizes their future because children will repeat this model, placing love for God and spouse after children. Remember, the sacramental covenant of marriage is eternal, forever binding a man and woman together by Jesus' unbreakable, divine love. Children placed before love of God or spouse will cause a marriage to suffer as parents' attention becomes too focused on education, sports and other extracurricular activities, putting their marital relationship on hold. Over the years, these couples grow apart, eventually realizing they no longer know or care about each other. They have become strangers. The research is consistent and overwhelming in numerous studies noting the soaring divorce rate when children leave home between their parents' eighteenth and twenty-fifth year of marriage. As adults, these spoiled, self-centered children who did not observe The Five Priorities of a holy, Catholic marriage and sacrificial love lived out in their families of origin, will themselves have difficult marriages, often questioning how long their parents lived a lie and whether there is authentic, lifelong love.

Finding time with a busy work schedule and the demands of raising a growing family is difficult. However, rather than trying to find time, make time for family prayer, communicate with each other and work together to keep The Five Priorities in the right order. Post the Priorities on the refrigerator or in a visible place so children can be reminded of their parents' love for God and each other. Explaining these changes to older children will help them understand the readjustment, allow them to feel secure in their parents' love as well as assist them in understanding the importance of a sacramental marriage and the deep love that exists between husband and wife. Extricating parents and children from numerous sports and other extracurricular activities will require time and effort and will not be easy. Setting up a gradual program of decreasing participation in multiple activities to a choice of one or two is often helpful as is readjusting the focus of family time in the evening and explaining the importance of reducing stress and chaos. Dinner can be made ahead of time on the weekend or put together in a Crock-pot before work. Dinner preparation can be a family event, with children helping, sharing the events of their day and experiencing less pressure from homework, study time and family prayer time. Just think, husbands and wives might even have a few minutes of quiet, peaceful time together to share their thoughts and feelings!

Share this with your spouse and live your *legacy of love*. Readjust disordered priorities to conform to The Five Priorities of a healthy, holy, Catholic marriage. Ask your spouse for help and work together to remain strong and vigilant. It is so easy to fall in with the culture, giving your lives over to hectic, chaotic schedules. Ask each other, "Who wants to derail our marriage and have our children abandon God?" We all know the answer. Fight back! Reduce external distractions. Have a place to park cell phones and other electronics in order to more fully focus on family; there can be a specific amount of time for them after dinner, dishes, homework and family prayer. What is "specific?" Recent studies note six or seven hours per day of various forms of electronics unrelated to school or homework is "average" for those between the ages of twelve and twenty-two! These same studies also note the resulting toxic effects upon the still-developing brain and recommend no more than one hour per day! Finally, keep in mind marriage and family are the school of love. If you teach love is service and self-donation, your children will learn the true meaning of marriage. Be the model of marriage your children will want to imitate. The time to begin is now: children grow up so fast and then they are gone!

Pick a Faith

"Jesus said to him, I am the way, and the truth, and the life; no one comes to the Father, but by me" (Jn 14:6).

We live in a secular culture that seeks to exclude God from our lives. We must be ever vigilant of the influences affecting our children's love of God, faith in Jesus and obedience to the Catholic Church.

One very popular, secular argument designed to turn children away from Jesus and His Church says children should be allowed to make their own decisions about what religion they will follow or whether to practice any religion at all! Of course, no one would allow a child to decide medical or dental care, inoculations, school attendance or obedience to society's laws: that would be bad parenting! But, to make a choice that has eternal significance . . . that is okay?!?

Our secular culture suggests children should have "space" and privacy to do their "own thing." The problem with this thinking is that it may catapult them into perversions, addictions, occult practices and all manner of sin. Satan loves secrets so there are no locked doors in a Catholic home. Computers are placed in a family area. Cell phones are placed in a bowl or basket by the door when everyone arrives home; they can be checked later in the family area. Parental controls on devices for teens are a must. Teens do not need social media. Their phones are for safety only. This is tough stuff but necessary for the health and well-being of our children!

As Catholic parents, we must teach the faith by modeling what we profess. We listen to our children with loving kindness, encouraging healthy behavior and forgiving poor decisions but instituting appropriate consequences for them. We attend Mass often as a family as well as the Sacrament of Reconciliation. Our Catholic faith is fundamental in providing a foundation for our children, stressing the development of strong moral judgment and individual powers of discernment. It is important our children see us pray as a couple and for us to pray with our children. Pray before meals and after the meal, pray a decade of the rosary.

What would we say about parents who are concerned with their child's diet, purchase the best and freshest ingredients, take extra care in preparation of the meal, serve it on fine china and then add a pinch of arsenic? What would we say when they wonder why their child becomes ill? We are composed of body, mind and soul. Each of these components need to be fed with healthy ingredients. The body needs nutrition, exercise and sleep; the mind needs to be challenged to learn the truth; and the soul needs a relationship with God. As Catholic parents, we are to teach our children through healthy, holy examples, supporting and nurturing them, providing love and understanding, so they will know their immense worth and value to God, to us and to their siblings.

The story about arsenic may seem silly but many Catholic parents dismiss the faith and their responsibility to teach it through words and action. Without a relationship with Jesus and the strength of sacramental grace to fortify them, Satan's arsenic can sicken children's souls, allowing them to participate in deadly sin. Parents send their children to the best schools, assist with homework, attend their sporting events, provide outstanding vacations, a wonderful home and neighborhood but intentionally cannot find time to pray, attend Mass, speak with love for Jesus and obey the Ten Commandments. They dispense with religious education unless it is time for a Sacrament and then identify themselves as Catholic. They never know or learn the differences between Protestant and Catholic beliefs but think it is great to learn about Eastern religions to broaden one's knowledge.

Whether it is arsenic on a plate or the arsenic of sin, the result is the poisoning of our children!

Children who have not been taught the Catholic faith or have not experienced the love of God modeled by their parents, struggle in discerning truth from error. They are deprived from knowing our loving God as well as the faith Jesus died to give us. These spiritually impoverished children are ill equipped for the spiritual battles they will encounter; they are like reeds blowing in the wind of error. Accepting secular thinking and cultural errors, they fall prey to ever-changing feelings, susceptible to the shallow offerings of life and unknowingly trade the eternal for the transient. They do not know how to pray because their parents never prayed with them.

A quick story: a professional, well-educated man was lamenting to a friend that his nineteen-year-old daughter had taken a "wrong turn," engaging in a relationship with a dangerous young man. He and his wife sent her to the best schools, provided for all her personal, educational and financial needs. Now, said the father, she was not listening to either parent but continuing in this unhealthy, dangerous relationship. Finally, the man's friend asked, "Did you pray for her as she grew up? Did you teach her to pray to God and obey His Commandments? Did you teach her how important her body is and that she needs to expect and demand respect, postponing sex until marriage?" The father replied he and his wife never thought of these things. Both were very busy with work while their daughter was busy with school and her activities. They decided she could pick her own faith when she was ready.

God's primary concern is that our souls one day return to Him. He has gone to a huge effort to have us understand His authentic love and desire for an intimate relationship with each of us. Yet, so many parents do not seem to make this a priority to teach their children, almost as if they cannot be bothered. God sent His only begotten Son to serve, teach and save mankind, entrusting His teachings to His Apostles to teach and carry the truth to all future generations. Would you agree that is important information for our children to know?

There are parents who would rather complain about the Church than make the effort to have God become their lifelong priority. They would rather say the Church is not pretty enough, cool enough, warm enough and that the priest is too old-fashioned in his thinking so they do not bother to attend Mass. They disagree over Church teaching but do not know Church teaching. They will not accept, agree to or take the time to learn Church teaching, instead listening to the anti-Catholic news so prevalent in the media! Their poor children are susceptible to all manner of errors because of their parents' laziness, focusing on the shallow, unimportant things of life and making little or no effort to address what is eternally important. Recall the importance of planting a sapling and supporting it with two stakes so it can withstand the wind and rain. As the sapling grows next to the two stakes, it bends less, becomes stronger and eventually supports itself. As Catholic parents, we are to be the stakes that support our children as they grow with strong, deep roots of knowledge, understanding and practice of the faith.

Share this with your spouse and live your *legacy of love*. Resist falling into the deadly sin of sloth, which can take the form of spiritual laziness in failing to be the spiritual guides your children need and deserve. Remember, as parents you participated in the act of co-creation with God; your children are created in God's divine image. You are to love them and instruct them about God as you live your love for Him through obediently following His will. Children are a great gift and a great responsibility. Parents are accountable to teach them as promised at their baptism. It is imperative that you use wisdom when making moral decisions, protecting them from all that can take them from the one, true, living, loving God. Pray with and for your children. If you do not teach your children to pray, who will pray for you when you are sick or near death?

School of Love

"Do all things without grumbling or questioning, that you may be blameless and innocent, children of God without blemish in the midst of a crooked and perverse generation, among whom you shine as lights in the world, holding fast the word of life, so that in the day of Christ I may be proud that I did not run in vain or labor in vain" (Phil 2:14-16).

God's plan is for parents to teach their children to know, love and serve Him through their thoughts, words and deeds, remaining close to the Sacraments, the source of grace given by Jesus to His Church. Parents teach and guide their family by living their love for Jesus, their spouse and their children through dedicated, selfless service. Unfortunately, due to Satan's attacks, the secular culture and free will, this perfect plan can be fraught with the hazards and consequences of sin.

The pressures of life can easily derail us from our most important task of loving God, our spouse and children. Falling into toxic patterns of behavior learned from our family of origin can quickly occur and we can unintentionally impart these hardwired behaviors to our children. In some cases, it can become generational sin, passed down from parent to child. Toxic behaviors can be deeply ingrained and transmitted as negative patterns, even sinful behaviors, from generation to generation. Providing correct modeling to our children is imperative but difficult in our present culture, especially if we are unwittingly fostering sin in our daily behaviors in the form of sloth, anger, jealousy, addictions or greed.

We are to be loving parents. Love is dying to self for another; it is hard work. If one wants the perfect image of love, sacrifice and dying to self, look no further than the crucifix. That is love!

As parents, we teach our children about God's love through our words and actions, having them understand they are a one-of-a-kind miracle created in God's divine image. We want them to know God has a very special plan for them in building up His Kingdom through their goodness and obedience to the Ten Commandments, prayer and sacramental grace.

Adults raised in toxic families can transmit patterns of anger, abuse and other sinful behaviors to the next generation of loved ones, perpetuating the hurt and pain. Please, stop the hemorrhaging! This is not how God intended the Sacrament of Marriage to be lived. We are the school of love and we are to teach our children how to love God first, our beloved spouse second and our family third.

We are all tempted to fall prey to deadly sins in small, incremental steps. That is Satan's plan: to entice us with the most minimal part of a deadly sin, knowing we may well seek a bigger fix, becoming more and more ensnared. We would do well to remember the Seven Deadly Sins and to remain aware of how easy it is to teach them to our children. When children are raised with anger, they become critical, abusive or depressed, rather than loving, kind and happy; when they are raised in a home that lacks peace, they may become complainers, jealous, envious and refuse to be charitable to others; when they are raised with laziness, they procrastinate rather than setting, working and achieving goals.

How can we help our children? We can begin with ourselves. Each spouse can acknowledge the negative behaviors and experiences they have been hardwired with from their family of origin that may be injuring their marriage and family. Next, we can listen to our spouse and focus on one behavior we have been asked to change. Do not argue! Accept what is being shared with a humble heart. Then, initiate a game plan. Questions are usually helpful. Clearly and specifically, what behavior is to be changed? What has been the usual, negative response? What emotions have followed the negative response? What are alternative responses? Which alternative responses could produce a healthier, more desired effect? Attend to the Sacrament of Reconciliation on a regular basis, sharing with Jesus, the Divine Physician, the incredible pain or deadly sins that continue to injure marriage and family. Ask God for a healing of the heart as well as the needed graces to end generational sin. Remain focused on changing toxic behaviors. The Sacraments are not magic, nor does the priest have a magic wand. We must be committed to changing our behavior and cooperate with the sacramental graces Jesus provides through His priest. Jesus' grace in the Sacraments is sufficient but not immediate. Be patient and kind with each other. Changing ingrained behaviors can take years, requiring the willingness to endure personal work, sacrifice and devotion to the Sacrament of Reconciliation as well as maintaining a specific, behavioral game plan for change. Growing in selfless love takes time but it is worth the effort for our spouse and children.

Share this with your spouse and live your *legacy of love*. Do not give up! Pray the rosary daily. Be persistent! Satan must not win. You must not give in to his lies and taunts that everything is really all right and it is just your unrealistic spouse who is asking for impossible changes! Your family loves you and they deserve to be loved by you. Continue to strive to live a faithful, Catholic life and marriage. This will lead to a more peaceful life and with God's grace, your children will be spared the pain you may have experienced as a child.

Domestic Church

"So then you are no longer strangers and sojourners, but you are fellow citizens with the saints and members of the household of God, built upon the foundation of the apostles and prophets, Christ Jesus himself being the cornerstone, in whom the whole structure is joined together and grows into a holy temple in the Lord; in whom you also are built into it for a dwelling place of God in the Spirit" (Eph 2:19-22).

St. Paul is speaking about the household of God, built upon the foundational teaching of the Apostles and prophets, handed down through Apostolic Succession and held true in today's Catholic Church. Christ gave His Apostles the Sacraments to strengthen and protect His followers until He returned. The Church has preserved these treasured Sacraments for two thousand years. Jesus continues to dispense the graces of His divine life in each Sacrament through the office of His priests. Catholic churches have an overwhelming, holy and peaceful feeling because of the presence of Jesus in the tabernacle and because of the holy sacrifice of the Mass. Catholic churches are pictorials, telling the story of the life, death and resurrection of Jesus through works of art such as stained-glass windows, paintings and mosaics. They also contain statues and relics of the great men and women whose historic, heroic love earned them the title, "Saint."

Just as our Catholic churches radiate the presence of Jesus, so should our homes radiate His loving presence. It is not enough to say we are Catholic; we must live Catholic. This means taking the Gospel message seriously; being Christ-like with our family, friends and those we encounter throughout the day. Living as Catholics means promoting love, peace, joy, forgiveness and understanding. Our homes are to be mini-churches in which virtue is lived daily. Catholic parents are to live the gospel of life and love within the home. The family is to be a community of persons who are faithfully living lives of sacrificial love.

Just as our Catholic churches contain beautiful art, so should our homes depict blessed art forms we call sacramentals. They are reminders of the lives of Jesus and Mary as well as favorite Saints and assist the family in focusing on their heavenly family and home. *"By the Church's prayer, they prepare us to receive grace and dispose us to cooperate with it"* (CCC 1670). Holy pictures, statues and crucifixes enable parents and children to reflect on the lives of the Holy Family, the Gospel accounts of Jesus and the early Church. It is not necessary to spend large sums of money on Catholic art. Pictures in most Catholic calendars are reproductions of beautiful masterpieces; they can be easily saved and framed when the month has ended.

Most importantly, a Catholic home reflects the love of Jesus and His Church by the attitudes and actions of the parents. Parents set the tone of the home with love, acceptance, gratitude, mutual respect, sharing, forgiveness, happiness, joy, prayer and peace. Teaching children Jesus' two great Commandments—loving God with our entire being and our neighbor as ourselves—is the foundation of our Catholic faith and family. Children learn Catholic teachings as they are lived daily through their parents' lives of prayer, love and self-donation for the betterment of the family. As time passes and they grow from childhood to adolescence to adulthood they will replicate this love of Jesus and His Church within their homes.

A Catholic home is not filled with verbal abuse, criticism, swearing, angry words or disrespect for God and family. Neither is it filled with rage, resentment, bitterness, jealousy, materialism, deceit, pornography or abuse of alcohol or other substances. Homes that are filled with these attitudes and behaviors will be unhappy dwellings. Children will not understand or believe in the love of God or charity to others if their home lacks love. Children learn what they live. If parents are observed as hypocritical Catholics, rarely attending Mass and living decidedly non-Catholic lives at home, children may decide they do not need or want God.

Closing the doors to our toxic culture is not easy but it is necessary even as the toxicity threatens to seep through every opening. As we have suggested, tuning out and unplugging from all forms of electronics during family evenings, except for a designated, short period, is important for reducing distractions. We mistakenly think we own our electronics but we are really slaves to our electronics. The addiction to television, computers, phones, ipads and social media is real, as we constantly check Instagram, Facebook or Snapchat. Adolescents and adults are never more than a foot away from their cell phones, even placing them on a nightstand or desk next to their bed prior to sleep. People undergo withdrawal, much as with drugs, if they are unable to remain connected every minute!

Finally, clean house of anything that is not of God. Our Catholic home and domestic church must be free of occult materials. Be especially aware of "gifts" given to children that may include books on witchcraft, tarot cards or Ouija boards. Such items have no place in a domestic church. Maintain an awareness of pornographic pictures, magazines or videos. Pornography and electronics have been labeled as the addictions of the twenty-first century. Overwhelming research concludes pornography is more difficult to remove from one's system than drugs: chemicals can eventually be expelled from one's body but images can remain forever. Over and over, we have heard men say their fathers introduced them to pornography as sex education and that this deadly misstep has become an addiction now destroying their marriage, preventing them from loving their wife as God intended. To one such man who was struggling with pornography he viewed on his computer, we suggested the ongoing Sacrament of Reconciliation where he could continually ask for and receive the graces needed to combat this addiction and to seek professional assistance. We recommended taking common sense precautions such as leaving his computer locked in the trunk of his car to reduce temptation, schedule time away from where he would most likely view pornography and instead schedule walks, rosary in hand, praying to our Blessed Mother.

Share this with your spouse and live your *legacy of love*. Do you speak kindly to your loved ones? Do your children feel welcome, safe, secure and loved in their home? Resolve to make your home a representation of the domestic church.

Try It, You'll Like It

"Beware of false prophets, who come to you in sheep's clothing but inwardly are ravenous wolves. You will know them by their fruits"
(Mt 7:15-16).

When their children are baptized, Catholic parents promise to raise them to know, love and serve God through faithful obedience to the truths of Jesus' teachings. With the Sacrament of Baptism, each child is adopted into God's family. The promises we make at our children's baptism are very real. One day, we will be held accountable for those promises. During the baptismal ceremony, the question is asked, "Do you reject Satan and all his pomp and works?" This is not an idle question: it is directed to us as parents to understand the battle we are in for our souls and those of our children. With baptism, we promise through our watchful and wakeful presence to protect our children with the understanding that God is placing them in our care for a period here on earth.

The Church on earth is called the Church Militant. Satan is always on the prowl; we must be ever vigilant. The assault on our families and children has become constant and insidious. Our secular culture considers any concept of Satan or a demon a silly superstition. However, aware of the destructive forces at work in our culture, it seems very evident Satan exists and his focus is the destruction of humanity by way of the family. For sixty years, slow, imperceptible changes have occurred simultaneously in education, electronics and the anti-God media, influencing all of us but especially our young. Our children's lives have been derailed and destroyed by premarital sex, rape, abortion, drugs, alcohol, abuse and domestic violence.

Catholic parents, beware! These are challenging times! We must remain alert and watchful as guardians of our children. We are at war with evil that is no longer acting in secret. Satan and his minions are at work in very obvious ways, excluding God and faith from our culture. Our Catholic identity is challenged every day. Wolves are at our door lying in wait, ready to pounce when the sheep are most vulnerable. We must remain aware of the secular ideas meant to seduce our children's souls. Statements such as, "Children should be exposed to everything so they can grow and learn from their experience of the world and not be sheltered" or simply, "Try it, you'll like it" are typical attitudes of our culture. We must counteract exposure to these cultural lies by teaching our children to engage in wise decision-making, discerning right from wrong, guiding them to grow in holiness, obedience and understanding moral consequences.

How can we, as Catholic parents, take these necessary steps?

First, begin to teach purity and modesty when children are two, three and four years of age rather than wait until they are teenagers. Girls learn from their mothers to dress, speak and behave modestly, so as not to be suggestive and bring unwanted, physical attention. Boys learn from their fathers the importance of respecting and protecting females to ensure their safety. Second, be vigilant, remaining aware of parental responsibilities as well as the very real dangers within the culture. Study neighborhoods and schools before purchasing a home. Consider homeschooling or Catholic education as a shield from negative, harmful influences. Be aware of peers influenced by the toxic culture who can become a conduit to danger. Do not presume every friend or neighbor is on the same track morally or that their children will not influence yours to experiment with alcohol, drugs or sex. Have a rule of no sleepovers. Arrange playdates or get-togethers at your home rather than sending them to houses of friends or classmates. Third, make it a priority to pick children up from school; this provides an opportunity to observe their friends. Meet with teachers to ask questions about books and classroom-learning materials to determine whether they foster a specific agenda. Read your children's textbooks! Fourth, be a positive role model. Teach love by words and actions; emphasize self-sacrifice and self-donation. Fifth, attend a weekday Mass as a family as well as on Sunday, with nightly recitation of the rosary, so children will see holiness in action while receiving the necessary graces to navigate the lies of our culture. Changing everything in your life to follow these suggestions will be nearly impossible: begin with one change then add another as time passes.

When we live our love for our spouse and work toward a holy marriage, we are not only protecting our children but also future generations. Our children, grandchildren and all generations to follow need to learn the truth about the love of God and Jesus' great and eternal sacrifice for each of them. See the big picture with the eyes and heart of God. We are often tired, perhaps stressing about job or finances. That is normal but we must remain focused on our Holy Catholic priorities and not lose sight of what is most important: love and devotion for God, our spouse and our children.

At times we will be given crosses to carry. During these difficult times, we turn to Jesus, have trust in His plan for us and ask Him to help carry our cross. We must not allow children to witness arguing or ugly confrontations. Instead, we offer the hurt and pain to God and use love, trust and peace to guide our beautiful family.

Share this with your spouse and live your *legacy of love*. As parents, you have been given a sacred trust. One day you will be accountable to God for how well you taught your children about Him and how well you protected them from physical, emotional, moral and spiritual evils. Therefore, it is important to pray constantly for them, pray with them as a family and talk to them daily about your love for God which must be lived out in obedience, prayer and the Sacraments that Jesus gave His Church.

Our Fourth Priority:

Work

IV

Our Fourth Priority:
Work

"Judge wisely the things of the earth and hold firm to the things of heaven" (prayer from the Second Week of Advent).

Initially, Adam was given the job of tending the Garden. After the fall, his work became toil, teaching discipline, obedience, self-control, perseverance, order and organization. Scripture gives many accounts of working Saints: Joseph was a carpenter, Paul a tentmaker, Luke a physician and Peter a fisherman. In the ancient monastic tradition, monks combined work with prayer to give glory to God. They understood the balanced combination of work and prayer controlled selfish tendencies and was essential to spiritual growth in service to the community.

Work is a gift, providing for the betterment and security of the family. However, like all gifts it can be misused, replacing the love of God, spouse and children for the love of success, greed, prestige and position. Deathbed realizations of a life misspent are painful. No one lies on their deathbed wishing they worked more or wishing they had made more money. Instead, they lament not spending more time preparing for the passing from one life to another, not loving God and family more and not spending more time with their beloved spouse. Suddenly, all the time spent in one's career or profession to the detriment of spouse, family and God appears meaningless and trivial.

However, if it is necessary to work long hours or even two jobs to have one's family survive in times of economic crisis then God bless you! That is not greed but self-sacrificing love. If one is in an all-consuming job, working long hours, it is important that time away from work be focused on the first Three Priorities.

There are certain jobs that require a great deal of time away from families such as the military, police, first responders and physicians working long hospital hours. These are all lifesaving professions that are also vocations. Society cannot live without these necessary jobs. It is important for spouses and children to be understanding of the commitment involved as these are part of a sacrificial life given to others.

Share this with your spouse and live your *legacy of love*. Assess time spent away from home while at work. Are you spending the correct amount of time at work for the correct reasons? Need to spend less time at work? Are you living within or beyond one's means? If your spouse voices a concern about the amount of time you are working and this time is interfering with living Priorities One through Three, then a readjustment may be in order. Your spouse is your first advisor. One of their major roles is to assist you in maintaining a balanced life to reach heaven by reminding you of your life's purpose. Listen with an open heart and refrain from angry responses. Always work together in the love and peace of Christ.

Financial Freedom or Financial Bondage?

"For the love of money is the root of all evils; it is through this craving that some have wandered away from the faith and pierced their hearts with many pangs" (1Tim 6:10).

The correct ordering of priorities calls for us to love God, serve people and use money. However, when materialism infects a culture, we ignore God, use people and love money. The love and worship of money then becomes similar to the pagan worship of idols.

Several years ago, we were preparing a couple for marriage. The young man was a financial planner, received a first-class education, worked hard, saved well, purchased a home for his future wife and was planning their wedding. He outlined his one, five and twenty-year financial plan. They were very much in love but continued to argue over some of the fancy items she was insisting on for their beautiful wedding. He was primarily responsible for the cost of the wedding and believed many of her wants were excessive and not in the original budget. Around and around they went. Finally, after admitting she struggled with self-control and self-denial, we asked about credit card debt. She broke into tears, sobbed and was unable to speak. They excused themselves, ending the session. He was shocked; she was mortified. The following week when we once again met, she explained she did have debt (huge debt, numbering in the very high five figures!) and that she had finally decided to share this with her fiancé rather than continuing to keep it secret. As a result, she was able to let go of a great deal of stress, guilt and shame. He was then able to help her set up a long-term plan to reduce and ultimately eliminate her debt. This new information threw his whole financial plan into turmoil but he was willing to make adjustments while she was willing to develop self-control and proper spending habits. His questions to her were, "Why did you not tell me in advance? When were you going to tell me?" She admitted she was afraid he would end their engagement and marriage plans. He assured her of his love but that she needed to be honest with him and trust his love . . . always! And the fancy items she was so insistent on having? They were no longer important as she now had something of far greater worth: his love, support and fidelity.

Another couple we were preparing for marriage came from very different socioeconomic families. He was from a family of modest finances who lived very simply. His entire life was a budget; he was adept at making do with what he had. His fiancé came from a wealthy family. She could purchase anything she saw and knew nothing of a budget. We asked them what each felt they could spend without discussing the purchase with their spouse. She said $2,000! He was shocked! His response was that every dollar needed to be discussed before being spent. They understood they came from different backgrounds but did not understand the impact of their family experiences on their spending habits. They needed to understand this could be a very difficult issue if they did not develop and work a mutually agreeable financial game plan. Coming from very different places and having different understandings of money and its use is a serious issue. Fortunately, they were willing to work together and created a sound financial game plan that satisfied them both.

We congratulate those couples who have been communicating openly and honestly about finances. For those who have yet to do so, we suggest beginning this process. Differences in socioeconomic background, similar or dissimilar spending habits, willingness to save, managing present expenses and deciding on future investments are all topics to be discussed sooner rather than later. It is also important to devote time to discuss immediate versus delayed gratification, avoiding the attitude of, "I want it now, so I'll get it now and worry about paying for it later." Do not fall for that dangerous, self-centered mentality. As spouses committed to a strong financial foundation, continue to work together to develop a sound, ongoing, mutually agreeable financial game plan.

When joined in a sacramental marriage, we give ourselves completely to each other. Nothing is held back; that would be selfish. Jesus died for His Bride, the Church. His sacrifice was complete and total. He held nothing back for His Bride to live. There is no backdoor: we are all in.

This brings us to a very divisive issue regarding finances. Does one spouse own and control the money? Financial possessiveness is unhealthy for a marriage, leading to division and discord. It also suggests the controlling spouse possesses the heart of a miser. In a healthy marriage, spouses share finances openly. Yes, one spouse may be the "breadwinner" but a primary purpose of work is to care for the needs of the entire family. It is not "my money because I earned it." When we married, we became a Sacrament, husband and wife devoting and donating ourselves to each other. We are aware of wives who have been forced to work and place their children in daycare because their husband would not allow them to buy anything without his approval. However, the husband felt free to do as he wished with the finances. In reality, finances are joint assets. Couples are to discuss the budget together, always behaving kindly and as generously as possible to each other. Spouses view their house, car and possessions as "our things." To say, "This is mine, I alone worked for it" is selfish, demeaning and controlling of one's spouse. The words "mine" and "yours" cease on the couple's wedding day. It's now "we," "us" and "ours." Finally, keep in mind, when both spouses work outside the home, it's still "our money," not "your money" and "my money." It's truly amazing what couples will and will not share!

An exception: when one spouse has a poor financial track record or if they have an addiction to reckless, financially dangerous spending, then it is important for their spouse to manage the finances. However, "manage" does not mean be secretive and leave your spouse without any knowledge of payment schedules or savings. How will they learn if their spouse acts like the controlling parent with a naughty child? Managing and paying the bills is never to be a secret with one's own, private password. What happens if the controlling spouse is sick and in the hospital or dies and the surviving spouse is unable to access their accounts? This happened to a young woman who was married to a very controlling man. He insisted it was his money as he had worked for it while she was home raising their three little sons. He gave her a tiny allowance to buy food and care for their children. Then one day he dropped dead at thirty-five of a massive heart attack and she could not pay for his funeral or food for their children because he controlled the money with secret passwords. Her family and friends had to step up and assist until the banks released the funds to her. At the funeral, she was unable to grieve: anger for having to borrow money to pay for the funeral and buy food were eating her up.

An essential component of a financial game plan should also address charitable giving. As Catholics, we are to tithe 5% to our parish and 5% to charities that support the Church and human life or 5% from our time and vocation. This is an important way for us to live our love for God and for others. We are simply stewards of the goods and blessings God has bestowed on us. Everything comes from God to us and then a small portion is returned to God and His people. It shows trust in God that we continue to work and pay the bills and it shows our obedient love for God and our fellow man. This is an important way to live our faith. Churches have huge expenses: staff, utilities and outreach programs to help our suffering, needy brothers and sisters in Christ. Remember Cain and Abel: Abel was generous and gave the first and best of his labor to God while Cain remained selfish and jealous, giving God a small, leftover portion.

Some people may debate the concept of charitable giving, saying, "God owns everything, so why do I need to give?" The answer as we have said is, "Yes, God does own everything except one huge thing. He does not own our free will." His love for humanity is so great, He gave us free will to choose to love Him or not, to trust Him or not, to be in a personal relationship with Him or to turn away and dismiss Him. What is important is our decision to use our free will to prove our love for God. The real question is not why we should give when God owns the world but what we can give back to God who has been so generous with us, beginning with His first gift to us: life. It was Cain who asked the age-old question, "Am I my brother's keeper?" Sadly, he thought not.

The real question in most people's mind is whether they can trust God to take care of them. Is God worthy of our trust? To answer that question, we must look at our lives and see that even though we have struggled and suffered, things do have a way of working out. Maybe not the way we wanted but we learned from the experience and grew because of it. All we need to do is look at a crucifix to know we can trust His love and mercy. No matter what suffering and trials we have dealt with or are still dealing with, it is important to acknowledge His gifts and graces. Looking at a crucifix reinforces for each of us the extreme suffering of Jesus, lived out because of His unconditional love for us. We can show our love by giving to those who suffer and are in need. This is a step each of us must take: to learn how good God is and how much He wants to take care of us if we will just trust Him.

Share this with your spouse and live your *legacy of love*. Many couples stretch their finances to give a false impression to others, wanting approval or admiration for accumulating material wealth or possessions. They buy the best house beyond their means or the best car beyond their means or the most expensive clothes beyond their means. Why? Could this be the sin of pride? Refocus on what is truly important. Have a sound financial game plan. Include giving to God, using free will to show love for Him by helping your church and those faceless, nameless people whose lives depend on your generosity. Finally, remember that when it comes to generosity, God will never be outdone!

Greed

"For you say, I am rich, I have prospered, and I need nothing; not knowing that you are wretched, pitiable, poor, blind, and naked"
(Rev 3:17).

To amass wealth, one must work very hard and remain focused on the bottom line to ensure financial success. The process of acquiring wealth occupies every thought, every minute of the day and night. Once wealth is acquired, there is the need to flaunt it by "living large" through many possessions. Eventually, the need to protect the wealth becomes a huge burden. Relying on a large bank account, a well-managed portfolio and wanting for nothing might seem admirable to most people, until they hear Jesus' words about their poor decision making by focusing all their energies on money. He never "sugarcoats" the truth. "Wretched," "pitiable," "poor," "blind" and "naked" are very uncomfortable words coming from Jesus. He wants us to understand it is our sinful, fallen nature and our greed that desire riches on earth. He wants us to desire the riches of heaven, which come from love and self-sacrifice.

Sometimes, people purchase coveted items without realizing the time needed for maintenance and protection of these sought-after valuables. Expensive purchases can own the owner, possessions completely taking over a person's heart, soul and life. This level of greed leads one to become the poorest of the poor, not realizing they lack the most valuable possession of all: a healthy relationship with God.

Such an individual has forgotten two important concepts. One, it is not a person's talent or brilliance that allows them to amass wealth but God. It is He who gifts us with our intellect, education and opportunities, planting the spark of an idea, allowing us to be at the right place at the right time or gifting us with the ability and strength to follow through with a laborious but necessary process. When one believes it is all about them, there is a failure to acknowledge the true, deserving source of success: God, who provided the necessary ingredients of timing, resources and imagination, bringing everything together at the right moment. Two, God desires to give all of us real wealth, the kind that does not perish. It is the gold refined in the fire of His love, service and sacrifice in which we conform our lives to Him, living the Gospel message and practicing our Catholic faith. Treasure in heaven is real treasure while treasure on earth is like fool's gold: bright and shiny but fake.

Often, when a person is constantly working and pursuing their career, time with spouse and family is greatly reduced. Relationships need time and attention for continued growth through shared experiences and reliance on one another. If one or both spouses are rarely or never home, their marriage and lives will suffer; they will depend on each other less and less for daily needs. In fact, both can become so independent they no longer need the other except for finances or sex. The working spouse is distant from the emotional, physical and spiritual needs of the family and, unfortunately, the family learns to get along without them. Of course, if the heavy workload is for a short duration or of immediate financial necessity, the family can plan and adapt accordingly, knowing it is a temporary situation.

We live in a wealthy country where most anything and everything is available for purchase. Unfortunately, "anything and everything" are distractions that cloud our mind and confuse our heart as to what is truly worthwhile. God becomes unimportant as materialism, self-indulgent pride and the desire for more money take over one's thinking and life. When this occurs, the family suffers as the ever-working spouse (or spouses) is rarely present to forge and maintain healthy, ongoing relationships.

Children growing up in this type of environment also struggle when it comes time to parent because of an absence of healthy role models.

When the focus of life is the acquisition of things, we become consumed and owned by materialism. Care of possessions occupies time and attention, leaving little or no time for reflection on God and prayer. Materialism is seductive. The media promotes lifestyles of the rich and famous with outrageous opulence, falsely leading people to believe riches lead to happiness. In actuality, the rich and famous often live sad lives filled with broken relationships, divorce and a host of chemical or alcoholic dependencies. Money and fame do not bring happiness, true love, joy or peace. Lottery winners often face bankruptcy, believing funds are limitless. Receiving money that was not earned can affect development of restraint, wisdom, self-control and deferred gratification.

In their last days, many people realize all they missed. Sadly, it is too late: time lost cannot be regained. They may be alone because of divorce or estranged from their adult children who now have very little time for their once absent parent. Yes, they supported their children financially but remained a complete stranger in so many other ways.

A true story of a man we both knew who worked so very hard at building his business: he held the purse strings very tight as his dream was to retire early. In fact, he was miserly. He left for work early and worked late every night. He had little joy and was consistently focused on his money and timeline for retirement. The children would need materials and assistance for a school project but he was unavailable. Christmas was meager; his children rarely attended birthday parties; a vacation was out of the question. Nearly every conversation with his wife was confrontational about the cost of utilities, food, clothes and registration for the children's sports activities and associated fees. Finally, he decided the time was right to sell his business. He met with a buyer who saw the potential for continued growth of this business and wrote out a huge check. His family was waiting at home, excited in the hope he would finally loosen the purse strings and, as a family, could enjoy time together. Time passed and a knock at the door revealed two policemen who regretfully informed them that the man suffered a heart attack while driving, causing his car to veer off the road. He was killed instantly with his uncashed check next to him.

Share this with your spouse and live your *legacy of love*. The husband and father in the preceding story planned on a nonexistent future. God is not in the past. He is not in the future. He is right now—in the present, identifying himself as "I AM." It is so sad to waste lives on dreams of the future instead of loving one's family today, not with extravagance but with the giving of time, attention and loving words to build up the body of Christ. Give thanks and appreciation to God for His many blessings in your lives, remembering to thank Him for His love, protection and guidance. Ask for the grace to live with contentment for the blessings and gifts He has given you and your family. It is also helpful to simplify your lives as much as possible by ridding yourselves of excess, buying only what is needed, paying off debts and living below your means. It is important to ask yourselves, "Do we need this or do we just want this?" Prayer, volunteering at a Catholic charity and the Sacrament of Reconciliation can all combat the deadly sin of greed.

Our Fifth Priority:

Everything Else

Our Fifth Priority:
Everything Else

*"Vanity of vanities, says the Preacher, vanity of vanities!
All is vanity. What does man gain by all the toil at which he
toils under the sun? A generation goes, and a generation comes,
but the earth remains forever"* (Eccles 1:2-4).

"Everything Else" refers to anything that takes us away from our first four priorities. The secular culture is very seductive, providing "opportunities" to derail us from living our priorities. They slowly creep into our lives, taking the form of electronics, movies, television, sports, gaming, acquaintances, hobbies or friends asking for constant time and attention. "Everything Else" can rule life and home, destroying peace and may include: an interfering relative who does not respect the boundaries of family; volunteering, which becomes the top priority; a controlling boss who does not respect family time; a best friend or fellow worker, married or not, inviting us to go out for drinks after work. We must be mindful of any person or activity that can take us away from living our first four Catholic priorities.

Our culture has so many distractions that intrude into our lives and steal time and attention away from the importance of correctly living the priorities of a holy, Catholic marriage. Today, everyone from the young to the elderly seem to have an electronic device in their hand every waking moment. Nonessentials rule our lives and time, pushing the eternally important farther away. Even people who are on track with their priorities find it hard to maintain consistency. There is always a distraction ready to derail us. We all know Satan is the great deceiver and the great distractor, seeking to derail us from our priorities, numbing our brains and souls, so that we become robotic, scrolling our thumbs and lives away. We must remain vigilant to his tactics!

Nothing is accomplished in life without planning. Presuming we will "just have the time" to live the first four priorities will not happen unless we are dedicated to scheduling time for individual as well as couple prayer. Check each other's schedule daily and decide when couple time will work. It may be meeting for coffee or lunch, arriving home early from work or walking after dinner and praying the rosary (we do so after dark when neighbors are less likely to interrupt). It is also important to plan on nights each week to get to bed early, close the bedroom door, discuss the events of the day, pray, have those conversations that there is never time for about your thoughts and dreams and then cuddle with each other.

When two people from large families marry, they form an even larger group that can become daunting. As the children marry and have children of their own, the group becomes a clan with almost constant celebrations. There are birthdays and anniversaries every month, leaving few weekends free for individual families. It becomes overwhelming as those who marry into a large family seek to have time alone with their spouse, immediate family and family of origin. Arranging one celebration each month for everyone with a birthday or anniversary is a system that can ease these difficulties. Other weekends can be left for one's own family, parents-in-law or to accomplish work around the house. Big families are wonderful but we have seen many couples burdened with celebrations and not have enough time with their own spouse and children.

Creating balance: one of the keys to a healthy, holy, Catholic marriage.

It is important for spouses to speak to each other and discuss social obligations and options prior to speaking to extended family members. If a topic needs more information before a decision is reached, research it, including perhaps speaking with a well-respected family member or one with experience on the topic. However, checking with our spouse to make sure we are both in agreement before sharing information that is personal or concerns one's immediate family is recommended. It only makes sense that speaking to another person without taking one's spouse into consideration will cause them to feel betrayed. We have often listened to a spouse express a sense of feeling 'blindsided" when told their spouse has discussed issues and reached resolutions after speaking with extended family members or friends without their spouse's knowledge or approval.

> **You are married.**
> **Your business is your business.**

Share this with your spouse and live your *legacy of love*. In every situation concerning change and growth you are to first consult with God through prayer and then with your beloved spouse through open, honest communication. Turn first to God, secondly to spouse. Talk about how to grow closer to God and each other always remembering you are a Sacrament. Altering or rearranging even one of the Five Priorities throws the entire balance off; relationships can then become at risk. Be vigilant about staying on track. Remind each other to schedule couple time and prayer time. Time does not just happen; it must be carved out, scheduled and planned. Are there distractions eating up time that have disrupted the healthy, necessary order of priorities? Review how time is spent on three or four typical days. Money and health can often be regained but time can never be recaptured. Wasting this commodity does not make sense. Help each other analyze the distractions that are keeping life off balance and stealing peace. Recommit to eternally significant priorities like praying with your spouse and serving each other.

In-laws and Outlaws

"For this reason a man shall leave his father and mother and be joined to his wife, and the two shall become one flesh. So they are no longer two but one flesh" (Mk 10:7-8).

Most Catholic parents understand the sacred nature of marriage that binds for life their adult child and their spouse to each other and Jesus and the importance of providing them with enough space and support to achieve a strong, holy foundation to their marriage.

Because of the time and effort to plan the many events of a wedding, it is easy to lose sight of what is taking place: a man and woman creating a new, separate family unit. This new marriage is to be respected as husband and wife are now a Sacrament bound together by Jesus' presence and love. They remain members of their family of origin but their roles have changed. Actually, on the couple's wedding day, everyone's role has changed! Having opened their homes and hearts in welcoming their adult child's spouse, parents and siblings are now looked upon to provide a supportive instead of primary role in the lives of the new couple who must now focus on growing and succeeding in their newly formed covenant. They need support from family and friends without unhealthy interference, opinions or manipulations.

However, some parents, busy with the excitement and plans of the wedding may not have fully processed their new role. They, along with siblings, may struggle with the change even presuming it is all right to "drop by" anytime without letting the newly wedded couple know in advance. Or, they may cling to the belief that their adult married son or daughter remains responsible in assisting with whatever they want, whenever they want.

It is important for the couple to explain The Five Priorities of a Holy Catholic Marriage to each of their parents prior to the wedding. Few parents, family members or friends should find difficulty with these priorities. Remember them?

1. **The First Priority is God, our ultimate authority.**
2. **The Second Priority is spouse, bound together in Jesus' love and unity.**
3. **The Third Priority is children, co-created with God, a gift from Him.**
4. **The Fourth Priority is work, essential for the provision and protection of marriage and family.**
5. **The Fifth Priority is everything else.**

Parents, other family members and friends are in Priority Five. However, understand this in no way undermines the love or respect of an adult child for their parents, family or friends. They continue to remain important but they are placed in their rightful order: only God, one's spouse, their children and work are more important.

The newly married couple do not abandon their parents or families of origin but remain an ongoing part of each other's lives. Most parents devote their lives to their children and may experience a sense of loss when they leave home, especially if they have enjoyed a healthy relationship. Although the relationship has changed, it can still retain the closeness they enjoyed prior to marriage. Loving and honoring our parents and our spouse's parents is lived by kind, respectful, caring behaviors toward them through phone or email, sharing of meals, celebrations of special occasions and get-togethers on a basis that works for everyone. If parents or parents-in-law need help, we should make ourselves available to the best of our ability and circumstances, keeping in mind our primary responsibilities. Both sets of parents ought to be treated with love, respect and understanding. When opinions are offered, adult children can listen, refrain from arguments and thank them for their interest, care and concern. We can all consider and learn from the insights and wisdom of our elders but that is not the same as allowing them to become the controlling center of our lives. As they age or need help, we can be attentive and present, keeping in mind what Scripture says about the care of a father being a sin offering.

It is interesting to note that both God the Father (Old Testament) and Jesus (New Testament) speak of the man leaving his parents rather than the woman leaving her parents. As always, God is right on! We have listened to couples—from newly engaged to those married for decades—detail their ongoing, toxic experiences with a manipulative, divisive, mean-spirited in-law who refuses to relinquish control of their adult child. In the vast majority of cases, the conflict is that of a mother refusing to relinquish her son to his wife. There is either a lack of communication from the mother-in-law to her daughter-in-law or an overabundance of hurtful, critical communication. Through tears, we have listened how a controlling mother-in-law makes it very clear that while her son and grandchildren are welcome in her home, her daughter-in-law is not! We have listened to situations of underlying jealousy and resentment in scheduling grandchildren's celebrations without first seeking their mother's consent as well as painful experiences of a daughter-in-law being excluded from family celebrations attended by her husband, his siblings, their spouses and children. Frequently the son's father is either mute or supportive of his wife as his daughter-in-law is being criticized as a poor wife and mother. However, the most damaging situations are those in which the son aligns himself with his mother in opposition to his sacramental spouse. Detailed conversations from his mother about how she is disrespected and ignored convince the son that an apology from his wife to his mother is needed. Often the son becomes angry, hurling abusive language to his wife as he continues to listen to untruths. In our experience, these situations can only be addressed when the son realigns his priorities and recommits to his sacramental marriage through spiritual guidance, a strong reliance on the Sacraments and ongoing professional assistance.

If parents have concerns about their adult child's future spouse, they can sit down and express them in a clear, succinct, kind, straightforward manner before the engagement begins. They can even suggest their adult child talk to their priest about his or her decision and seek professional consul. Throughout the engagement they can be there to help their son or daughter discern if this is a good candidate for marriage. Having a kind but serious dialogue about the most important decision their child will ever make is certainly appropriate. However, if their adult child remains firm in their choice of a spouse, the parents should make every effort to be welcoming, supportive parents-in-law. Adult children may well decide to marry someone of their choice versus their parents' choice. It is their life and hopefully the parents have provided the necessary tools throughout their child's life to make a healthy decision.

With regard to the relationship of the infamous mother-in law and her new daughter-in-law, it would benefit jealous or controlling mothers-in-law to remember it is the mother who raises her children and not the grandmother. God ordained this job in Genesis when He said Eve was to bear children. It is the mother who carries and bears the child. Fathers are involved and their role is obviously important but their primary job is to protect and provide. They live their love for their wife by assisting her in the raising of the children as she knows them best. The father learns about childrearing from his children's mother and takes cues from her. It is important for parents-in-law to be their new daughter-in-law's support team. Volunteer and say "yes" when asked to help or assist. Treat her as a daughter, loving and praying for her and the sacramental union she shares with your son. Be the model of love. She will gain a better understanding of the nature of Catholic marriage as one of self-donation as she experiences your service and sacrifice for her sacramental marriage. This is Catholic love in action!

Share this with your spouse and live your *legacy of love*. Do parents and/or other family members need, with sensitivity and kindness, The Five Priorities explained? Ensure their behaviors do not cause arguments and unhappiness between you and your spouse. It is your responsibility to be kind and loving to your parents and parents-in-law but to always support your spouse so that all may see you are one, a unified Sacrament.

Diversions and Distractions

Diversions and Distractions

The World We Live In

"Whoever causes one of these little ones who believe in me to sin, it would be better for him if a great millstone were hung round his neck and he were thrown into the sea" **(Mk 9:42).**

In the 1950's, our society adhered to the Ten Commandments. Intact families shared meals, talked with each other, prayed together and attended church as a family. Rather than live alone, a grandparent would move in with their adult child. Mothers and often a grandparent were home during the day. Neighborhoods were safe and doors unlocked. Fathers worked to support their families. Children were raised to love God and respect authority. Parents depended on schools to provide a sound, healthy education. People worked out their marital issues behind closed doors. Infidelity and divorce were for Hollywood movies and the rich and famous. By the end of the decade, everyone owned a television. Hollywood and the media meant mass influence leading to new, rebellious ideas, culminating in moral relativism and secularism together with the notion that the Ten Commandments and the Catholic Church were offensive and repressive. Radical feminism "empowered" women to reject pregnancy and family for careers while artificial contraception promoted promiscuity and infidelity. Educators and mental health professionals advocated freedom for children from tyrannical, parental rule. Planned Parenthood was invited into children's schools to teach sex education and to encourage children to express themselves sexually.

The culture did not understand the real threat of a spiritual vacuum. When school prayer was banned by the relentless work of militant atheists, the destructive evils of drugs and weapons entered schools. New Age, Eastern paganism became popular, lacking rules for protection but promoting self-awareness which was often code for, "Do as you please to be at peace or make yourself happy." Music festivals introduced free love and mind-altering drugs. TRUTH was replaced with opinions. These changes eventually contributed to infidelity, divorce, multiple marriages, rape, pornography, sexually transmitted diseases, perversions, recreational sex, abortion, recreational drug use, addictions and social violence.

The physical, emotional and moral trauma to families has been a tsunami of historic proportions. This devastation has wrought changes on once normal, healthy, law-abiding families and can be compared to the overwhelming transitions thrust upon the population during the Industrial Revolution, the Civil War, the Great Depression or one of the World Wars.

Like a wild animal, Satan attacks the most vulnerable. As a predator, he waits hidden, watching for the youngest, smallest or weakest to be separated from the herd and then pounces on the unaware prey. In Scripture, Jesus speaks to us about how to remain strong when Satan tempts us but we do not always pay attention. Satan presumed Jesus, after His forty-day fast, would be susceptible to temptation, thinking He was physically, mentally and emotionally exhausted. He may have been but He was spiritually strong, having fasted and prayed to His Father. Jesus repelled Satan. Our culture has become spiritually weak. We have ceased to pray and have difficulty remembering and living Jesus' commandments of love. We have fallen prey to Satan and his human minions in their goal to weaken marriage and family, seeking to remake the image of God on the human souls with his broken, bent, sinful image.

In the parable of the wheat and the weeds, Jesus reminds us of the necessity of constant vigilance. While the good landowner is asleep, the enemy plants weeds in the field of wheat. This is a story for every age to take seriously as Satan continues to successfully target his unsuspecting prey. When families become splintered, communication becomes greatly reduced and the contemplation of God, faith and the protection of prayer ceases. It then becomes ever so easy for Satan to work his duplicitous tactics. Overindulgent materialism leads to frequent arguments between spouses as materialism is viewed as an important, worthwhile goal and expensive homes and cars become status symbols. Watching television in bed at night keeps couples exhausted, thwarting genuine couple time and communication.

Because parents were overwhelmed, constantly overextended and too busy to raise their children, children began to raise themselves or were enrolled in after-school programs. They were taught to confide in school counselors as their parents were busy and too old-fashioned to understand it was normal for children to experiment with sex, alcohol and drugs. As crazy as it sounds, counselors and school nurses could not dispense aspirin for headaches but they could counsel a teenager to receive birth control pills, condoms or an abortion without their parents' knowledge!

For those parents with small children, the business of childcare became a huge industry. It was expensive and a "mixed bag" with respect to quality of care. Most were staffed with excellent, compassionate, well-trained professionals but others were unqualified, looking for easy money or an opportunity to abuse children. At the very least, children were exposed to health issues, negative behavioral situations and disrespectful, crude language repeated at home. Some parents rethought the idea of the mother working outside the home, made the decision to live more simply and raise their children in a more conventional, traditional manner.

Other couples decided that the wife would continue her

career with the education and training received in her college years. Do not misunderstand: it is very important for women to be as educated and successful as possible. Time, effort and money spent on securing an education are to be taken seriously. We have worked with couples where it was necessary for the wife to resume her career because of her husband's chronic illness. Nevertheless, expectations for their future as wives and husbands as well as exactly who is going to raise and influence their children remain important issues for couples to discuss. Ideally, discussions on these life-impacting decisions should begin before marriage. It is helpful to discuss flexibility in career options, professions that can be accomplished from home, jobs that can be shared with another individual or ones allowing flexible scheduling to accommodate the needs of one's family. Assistance from trusted family and friends is also a viable option to aid in safe childcare. Consider this process as the most important set of interviews one will ever conduct: the decision as to whom a person marries will impact not only the rest of their lives but that of their children.

> It is never a good idea to fly by the seat of one's pants when raising children who are a gift from our most loving, generous God.

We recently worked with a couple preparing for marriage. He was from a traditional family with a stay-at-home mother while her mother was completely career focused. The young lady told the story her mother had proudly imparted to her many times: "My mom always said, I had an excellent education and an important career. Anyone can raise a child but few can achieve my position in the corporate world. So, two weeks after giving birth, I dropped you off at daycare. Everyone at work was most amazed and impressed at my level of professionalism and dedication. My story was always told to other young employees who became pregnant and expected lengthy time off." The young bride-to-be said that she, too, would be following in her mother's footsteps. Her fiancé looked at us with such sadness; he wanted her to be with their babies and enjoy motherhood. As our sessions progressed, we talked more and more about the gift of children and their immortal souls. Finally, one week she broke down, began to cry and shared that she never felt loved by her mother. She was only given attention when she was successful at school or sports. She never felt loved for herself. Even now, she said her mother kept urging her to continue to work and focus on moving up in her company. She said, "I actually hate the choices my mother has made and I'm struggling with my love for her. I see how great my mother-in-law-to-be is with her children and grandchildren and I want that kind of love in our home." We continued to work with them for another three months until they left for the East Coast because of her husband's job transfer. Several years later, she gave us a call saying she had three little girls and was very, very pleased that she and her husband had created a game plan for her to be a stay-at-home mother!

Share this with your spouse and live your *legacy of love*. The world we live in no longer embraces God, marriage and children as the highest priorities. It is up to you to remain vigilant and focused on protecting your family. Remember: television and especially internet access should be in the most visible and public part of the house rather than in children's bedrooms. Periodic monitoring of content is also a good idea. Outside influences have a huge, negative effect on marriage and families. Be aware of what your children are learning through electronics as well as in school. Strive to teach them the faith through positive examples. Pray as a family with your spouse and children every night.

Don't Be Duped

"Therefore take the whole armor of God, that you may be able to withstand in the evil day, and having done all, to stand. Stand therefore, having fastened the belt of truth around your waist, and having put on the breastplate of righteousness, and having shod your feet with the equipment of the gospel of peace; besides all these, taking the shield of faith, with which you can quench all the flaming darts of the Evil One. And take the helmet of salvation, and the sword of the Spirit, which is the word of God" (Eph 6:13-17).

The 1960's began an avalanche of cultural and social change. The relativistic, materialistic and atheistic engineers of social change slowly removed and replaced our country's Judeo-Christian belief system with secular humanism. Man excluded God, installed himself as his own god, reduced truth to a subjective idea and made himself the center of being and importance. The entire concept of religion, including the Ten Commandments, God, Jesus, Satan, heaven and hell was considered a silly superstition held over from the Dark Ages. The unique importance of each human being bearing God's image within their immortal soul as well as the accountability for choices resulting from free will was also considered silly and unimportant. The intellectual elite erroneously believed that if they could get rid of God and the "thou shalt not" rules, everyone could be at peace and live happy lives doing as they pleased with no God to judge them. *Time* magazine's cover read "GOD IS DEAD."

Who are we to believe?

Are we to believe Jesus, who proved Himself trustworthy through a life of words and deeds? He was prophesied throughout the Old Testament, fulfilling all that was written. He said He was the Son of God and proved it. He lived a life of miracles,

118

raising the dead, curing the sick, walking on water and calling upon nature to obey Him. Even Satan, after Jesus' fast in the desert, approached Him and identified Him as the Son of God, taunting and testing Him. Jesus taught and lived a life of love and peace. He founded His Church on twelve men, teaching them and giving them the authority and power to carry on His work. He foretold His death. Hanging from His cross, He forgave His executioners. After three days in the tomb, He rose from the dead. Five hundred friends—"brothers"—saw Him after His resurrection. Finally, He ascended to heaven. Jesus said His name is TRUTH. He showed us Satan and his demons were real, frequently casting them out of those possessed, the demons calling out to Jesus and identifying Him as the Son of God. In each case Jesus cast them out, returning the possessed person to full health.

Who are we to believe?

Are we to believe the secular thinkers of our current age who make a name for themselves and become huge media personalities, becoming wealthy on their books and movies, basking in the limelight of notoriety? Are we to believe the social, atheistic architects who slowly and imperceptibly seduce an unsuspecting American culture into accepting the Seven Deadly Sins as "rights" replacing the Fruits of the Holy Spirit?

It is really not that difficult who to believe . . . is it?

Satan does not act on his own. He has an accomplice: weak mankind. The very creature God has poured all the gifts of love into has a fallen nature because of the first sin of rebellious disobedience. Satan dupes us to engage in one or more of the Seven Deadly Sins as an opportunity to use our free will to choose evil instead of good. Over and over, he looks for our weakness to a particular sin, presenting it to our fallen nature and free will as an innocent idea to act upon. Every one of us possess weaknesses and being duped to accept and act upon the deadly sins is the cause of so much pain in our world.

When entering a war, a country studies the enemy and their tactics. They arm the fighting force with the necessary training and equipment to protect them and achieve victory. Unfortunately, in letting go of God, Jesus' teachings and His Church, we were ill equipped to battle the forces of sin "loosed" on our culture. However, Jesus said He would never leave His Church. We must turn to deepening our relationship with Him. The only way to defeat the power of evil presently infiltrating our culture, our lives and those of our families is to cling to the Sacraments Jesus gave us that contain the divine graces and spiritual help needed to assist us in this battle with evil. Satan is a created being who chose to war against the all-good, all-loving God because of pride and refusal to serve or obey. Satan cannot injure God. What he can do is attack God's precious children made in His divine image. Satan is strong but we are stronger when armed with the Sacraments, prayer and obedience to Jesus' teachings, living lives of humble service and love.

In our marriages, we must guard against petty arguments, disagreements, conflicts and hurt feelings designed by Satan to trick us into fighting with our spouse. So much conflict has a basis in one of the Seven Deadly Sins but pride is usually the root cause: "My way, my money, my ideas . . . I deserve that . . . I'm right . . . I'm angry with you, I'll get even . . . I won't say I am sorry, it's not my fault." Satan manipulates couples into angry arguments, fights and hurt feelings. Arguing and refusing to cooperate with our spouse puts us in a very dangerous place. No one wants to be duped but that is exactly what we allow to happen when we let Satan provoke us into fights and arguments with our beloved, arguments that are so often based on pride, self-love, fear, getting even and hurt feelings.

When Gary and I were married, we looked quite perfect and compatible on paper. All the boxes were checked: we loved each other very much, came from intact, practicing Catholic homes, were college graduates and Gary had just completed his Master's Degree. What could go wrong? Well . . . a great deal went wrong! We were both strong, type "A" personalities, unwilling to bend or give. We argued and fought a great deal. Years went by and we were not happy. But as we grew closer to the Sacraments, we began to realize Satan, God's enemy, was also our enemy. We slowly began to rely on the Sacrament of Reconciliation and the rosary to effect change. Now, when we work with couples in marriage mentoring, we explain that we have been where they are and we know it can get better. One of the most important concepts we have learned is to recognize that when we were entrenched in a disagreement, not willing to give in, one of us would finally realize who had entered the room and say, "Honey, let's stop. We know who is present and we're being duped." Acknowledging Satan's presence diminished his power. He is sneaky but when discovered and called out, loses his edge. We were no longer willing to fight each other so Satan lost.

> **We are not really fighting our spouse.
> We are really fighting Satan.**

Share this with your spouse and live your *legacy of love*. Calm down! The real enemy is rarely our spouse. Let us refocus by dedicating ourselves to living our love for God through increased prayer and the Sacraments. We can then live our love for our spouse by serving with genuine love and self-sacrifice. We can also change the habits and behaviors that are causing many of the present issues, taking responsibility for hurt caused to our spouse. Finally, we can attend the Sacrament of Reconciliation, confessing pride and selfishness, asking Jesus for His and our spouse's forgiveness as well as for the graces to make amends. Every day we must remain vigilant so as to not be duped by Satan.

Discord and Divorce

"So they are no longer two but one. What therefore God has joined together, let no man put asunder" (Mt 19:6).

Jesus was clear about divorce. However, our toxic culture no longer appears to care about Jesus' words. Instead, the lie is promoted that love should be fun, always feel good and when love becomes work, well . . . it is time to leave! This has resulted in serial relationships, broken promises, insatiable lust and the victimization of women and children. Catholics must be aware of and protect themselves from this mentality. The sacramental nature of Catholic marriage means a man and a woman freely present themselves to Jesus and His Church on their wedding day, pledging a sacred vow to be faithful, fruitful and remain within a permanent, exclusive unity for life. Jesus becomes a part of their lives in an unbreakable covenant bound together by His eternal love. A secular wedding is a contract between two people; contracts can be broken. A covenant cannot be broken because it is between husband, wife and God. God is faithful: He never breaks His promise.

Every couple that walks down the aisle is presumably in love. However, after a breakup either or both may say, "I fell out of love." They may end up wondering if love even exists, whether it is nothing more than just a fleeting, romantic feeling. As we have said, Satan is at constant work to destroy marriage and families. He especially sets his sights on sacramental marriages, because we are supposed to be teaching others how to live their love as "light" and "salt" to the world. He wants to spread the lie that Catholic Sacraments have no power. He seduces couples into believing that God, who is love, does not exist in an effort to separate husbands and wives from believing in God, the Sacraments or marriage. The result of Satan's efforts: the many young married adults raised in a home who witnessed the slow, painful dissolution of their parents' marriage. As problems occurred, their parents may have sought counseling. If they went to a secular therapist who may also have been divorced, they would be encouraged to move on and find love elsewhere. Although their parents fervently desired to remain married and vowed divorce would not be an option, as children, they never saw their parents endure and work through rough times nor did they observe or learn strategies of healthy communication, patience, sacrifice and commitment. Instead they sadly concluded, "Wow, mom and dad were right, love does not last and marriage is impossible."

Divorce is unhealthy for spouses, signaling the death of love, history, hope and dreams for their future together. This results in discouragement, depression and possibly affairs separating them from God. It is also unhealthy for their children as they can become pawns between parents and learn early that love is an empty promise. Many children are then exposed to their parents' new "live-in" relationships and it would not be unusual if these transient "live-in lovers" physically or emotionally abuse the children.

Husbands and wives wonder: "Where did I go wrong?" "Weren't we in love?" "We were so happy in the beginning, what happened?" There is usually more than one answer to these questions but a couple's early history, together with a dysfunctional culture is usually a primary reason. A man and woman meet as young adults and rush into an intense sexual relationship with little knowledge or understanding of their partner's personality, family history, personal issues, expectations regarding finances, religion or lifestyles. Exciting sex forms the core of the relationship. They are among friends who repeat the same pattern: meeting someone, feeling lust, engaging in casual sex, finding enjoyment in similar activities, moving in to save money and moving out when the fun ends. This has led to the destruction of permanent relationships and the stable, healthy family generating love, approval and acceptance. How can a culture thrive if families do not?

The giving of one's body is a highly treasured, special gift of intense love and devotion for life. It is something precious, intended for one's spouse on their wedding night when they are bound together for life, physically, emotionally, mentally and spiritually. Too often, however, the precious gift of one's body is given to others as part of a temporary, fun relationship. There is no regard for the importance of the sacred dignity of one's body, heart, mind and soul. Instead of protecting this gift, it is misused over and over. Both the man and woman may have engaged in several of these relationships prior to marriage, beginning as a teen and continuing through young adulthood. Serial dating consisting of a "fun, lust, sex, hurt, breakup" routine became ingrained, forming a pattern of selfish behaviors planting seeds of future, destructive divorces. Such individuals become overwhelmed when the thrill of new romance and fun fade and they are faced with the reality of working in cooperation with another. They are asked to change annoying or destructive behaviors, actually work individually on their marriage, sacrifice, serve another and remain committed to their spouse as they vowed. Many times, the response is, "Wow! Too hard!"

> **A healthy marriage depends on God's design, not man's design.**
>
> **A healthy marriage depends on God's rules, not man's rules.**

When couples become angry, they often say things they do not mean because they are hurt and want to return the hurt. As the argument and angry words escalate, one spouse may threaten divorce. Now the other spouse, refusing to be threatened, will battle back with, "Fine, I'm done too. You can pack your bags or I'll pack mine and get out." What began as an argument has escalated because of frustration, hidden hurts and the difficulty of living responsibly and sacrificially. Now we have two determined people who want to quit. Normally, spouses would rarely bring up the "D" word but in the heat of an argument divorce is threatened. Sometimes one or both spouses are so hurt and angry they are certain someone (anyone!) would be better than their spouse. All they know is they are done and want out. We have heard many times that a spouse left over an argument that escalated beyond control. Neither would initiate reconciliation as both were stuck in pride. One woman that we worked with said she realized she threw away her husband who eventually found another woman. She had been blinded by anger and self-vindication, presuming he would come back and apologize. Too late, she realized she should have taken the initiative. Neither friends nor family made the effort to talk Catholic sense to her.

Share this with your spouse and live your *legacy of love*. Satan sows seeds of discord and divorce. Do not be seduced into his game by allowing the notion of divorce to enter your thoughts when frustrated or angry. Do not be seduced into the battle being waged against the true meaning of marriage, holiness and family. If divorce has entered your thoughts, meet Jesus in the Sacrament of Reconciliation and ask Him to give you the graces to love your spouse as you vowed on your wedding day and then increase your prayer life. Sacrificial love is the love Jesus has for you. Honor Jesus' love for you by loving your spouse sacrificially even when they are not lovable or loving to you. Make it a priority to love and serve your spouse.

Indoctrination

"Whoever receives one such child in my name receives me; and whoever receives me, receives not me but him who sent me" (Mk 9:37).

Jesus' words are clear: a culture that does not welcome children is a culture that does not welcome Jesus or His Father! Accepting Jesus is being open to life, open to understanding we are all created in God's image. His greatest blessing to us as a couple is fruitfulness, allowing us to co-create with Him in conceiving and bringing forth the miracle of new life. As parents, we are then responsible to participate in the shared responsibility to love and teach our children about the love and faithfulness of Jesus and God, our Father.

Of course, love of children is not Satan's plan. Hating God and obedient love, he searches for ways to stop the faithful, fruitful love of husband and wife and the love for new life. The internet, television, movies, books and magazines indoctrinate us with negative concepts about pregnancy and children. Many in the media have equated children with a disease. We are told the world is too dangerous to bring a child into or they are too expensive to raise, derailing our desire for travel and the finer things of life. We are also fed the lies that children will "use up" all our natural resources, be undisciplined, complicate our careers and interfere with our desire for leisure. The conclusion? Children are just too much of a burden! Additionally, the medical and scientific communities offer a plethora of drugs and other contraceptive tools to allow for frequent sex without the "disease" of children, now devalued from one of God's greatest gifts to a curse. Satan has appealed to our selfishness and our lustful concupiscence as proud rights. Children are no longer accepted as a gift made in God's own image with an immortal soul but rather a mass of protoplasm, originating from pure chance. What lies!

Freedom to have sex without love, devotion or commitment

gives one control without personal or financial responsibility. Our government has even become part of this process, paying for aborting an "accident" and promoting fears of overpopulation and lack of proper living spaces. However, flying over our continent or any of the other continents, we would clearly observe the vast, empty, open stretches of unpopulated land! Most populations reside in urban areas, comprising only a fraction of land. God said to go forth, "Be fruitful and multiply." He did not say to do this just until the 1960's, when the birth control pill and the sexual revolution hit the culture like a tsunami!

Our culture has replaced faith in God with faith in people who control the media, education, government and science. We have turned away from obedient love of God, dedication to families and respect for life. We have turned toward disobedience and dismissal of God, rejection of marriage and family and the devaluing and disrespect for life. Satan uses subtle, almost imperceptible changes so we will not recognize evil and reject it. Remember the story of how to cook a frog? If the frog is placed in hot water, it recognizes the danger and hops out. However, if it is placed in cool water and the temperature increases slowly, it adjusts and remains in the hot water until boiled!

In the Declaration of Independence our forefathers declared, *"We hold these truths to be self-evident, that all men are created equal, that they are endowed by their Creator with certain unalienable Rights, that among these are, life, liberty and the pursuit of happiness."* It is no coincidence that the first freedom mentioned is life: if one is denied life then one can never achieve liberty or pursue happiness. When the option of life is taken away, all other rights cease to exist. Sadly, we have denied life to millions of babies for over forty years and created millions of mothers who mourn their unborn child's death.

When we replaced faith and belief in God with faith and belief in people and machines, we placed ourselves in harm's way. Self-discipline and personal responsibility were replaced by the license to do whatever we pleased. The "pursuit of happiness" became the only important freedom to many in our culture, portrayed over and over as our primary right regardless of cost. Sociology has long taught that a bloodless coup can be orchestrated by controlling two sectors of the culture: first, the media, through subversion of truth by constant bombardment of false information; and second, the indoctrination of our children through secular, materialistic education. With the media indoctrinating adults and state education indoctrinating children, the focus of a culture can be turned away from God, faith and family, replaced by new methods to disrupt and destroy faithful families, love and respect for life.

Respect for life can be found in Natural Family Planning (NFP), a natural way of emphasizing communication between spouses, self-control, cooperation and abstinence while being open to life. God wants us to plan our family through prayer, learning our beloved's fertility cycle, abstaining when she is ovulating and being open to even the unexpected pregnancy, accepting that God's plans are not always our plans. Spouses who practice NFP report a deeper, more intimate level of communication together with increased spiritual and emotional intimacy. This means loving each other through tender, nonsexual cuddling; both knowing and agreeing they need to refrain from sex until their spouse is no longer fertile, always communicating and working together. Jesus said, *"The thief comes only to steal and kill and destroy; I came that they may have life, and have it abundantly"* (Jn 10:10).

Our culture encourages a lack of self-control, especially toward sex. There is no communication about the woman's body and the need for her to take an unnatural birth control pill that may often affect her health. We would do well to remember that God is the life giver while Satan is the life killing, destructive thief. Human life is so important to God that He sent His only Son to live a human life and die a human death so that we could have eternal life with Him.

Our once-healthy culture has become toxic, blindly rejecting two of the exclusive gifts granted to a husband and wife: holy sacramental marriage and the fruitfulness of the divine image. We have too easily accepted the false concept of privacy, forgetting our Creator, Almighty God, is ever-present, seeing and knowing all. *"For the word of God is living and active, sharper than any two-edged sword, piercing to the division of soul and spirit, of joints and marrow, and discerning the thoughts and intentions of the heart. And before him no creature is hidden, but all are open and laid bare to the eyes of him with whom we have to do"* (Heb 4:12-13).

Share this with your spouse and live your *legacy of love*. Life becomes easier when you follow the Ten Commandments as your template for life. You will create fewer problems for yourselves when disciplined and follow the teachings of Jesus and His Church. Resolve to tune out the lies of our culture. If you have listened to them, misused the gift of sexuality and have not been open to life, it is time to choose the Sacrament of Reconciliation . . . begin anew. Contact Natural Family Planning and learn about their program; it is as effective as artificial contraception but far safer, completely natural and with the additional benefits of teaching discipline, communication and true intimacy between spouses. Remain close to the Sacraments so Jesus may guide and protect you and your family with the graces of fortitude and wisdom. God is calling you and your spouse into a deeper relationship of loving, trusting and obeying Him. Answer His call!

Of the World

"If you were of the world, the world would love its own;
but because you are not of the world, but I chose you out of the world,
therefore the world hates you" (Jn 15:19).

In a culture of secularism and relativism devoid of God, people become their own god. They decide the rules by which they will live, free to change or break them as situations and circumstances dictate. Morality is mocked, personal accountability, right, wrong and permanence of justice abandoned. Life becomes a series of escape hatches: "If this doesn't work, I'm out of here! If the plan no longer serves me, I'll change it!" Jesus warns us to remain aware of worldly people who inhabit every layer of society, following their individual whims rather than God's laws for His perfect plan. We, as Catholics, need to remember that when everyone around us is making their own rules and following their selfish longings and lustful behavior, we are not to follow in their footsteps but instead follow Jesus' words and the teachings of the Church He founded on His Apostles.

At an early age, we accept rules in sports like, "Three strikes and you're out." Can you imagine if one batter said, "No, I want five strikes before I'm out!" Those who are "of the world" are angered that our loving God dare give us rules for our well-being. To get rid of God's rules, people get rid of Him by denying His existence and His ten rules of love and protection. In this toxic environment, we are to live vigilant lives of faithful, loving obedience and trust in Jesus as we protect our marriage and families.

Recall Jesus' parable about the weeds and the wheat. The workers wanted to tear out the weeds but the good landowner allowed them to grow together and at harvest time ordered the workers to gather the wheat and throw the weeds into the fire.

Of course, the landowner is God. He has planted us to do His holy will and be tested in a world that will scoff at us, make our lives difficult because of our beliefs and finally reject us. Just as weeds in a garden never stop choking the life out of beautiful plants, those who hate God and His creation never stop attempting to choke the life out of our faith and those who follow God. They seek to remove the Ten Commandments from government buildings and prayer in schools. In contrast, lawlessness, witches and the demonic are embraced as right and good. Secularism embraces every sexual act and every degrading sin with thinking such as, "I'm okay, you're okay, anything we choose is okay." Those who choose to live in obedient love of Jesus are hated while those who embrace all possible lifestyles are loved and revered in the culture. What rubbish!

The early Church lived in pagan times but remained faithful. We now live in a new era of paganism; it is our duty to protect our families in this new war against God. Satan continues to seduce mankind, sowing seeds of hate and destruction. Moreover, he offers the temptation of sexual immorality, knowing it will lead to the destruction of human life, especially the killing of innocent, unborn children and wound millions of women. Satan has spent two thousand years trying to destroy the Catholic Church and his minions will continue their attempts at destruction. However, we do not need to be filled with anxiety over Satan's evil works. Jesus commissioned His Church and Apostles—His only legitimate teaching authority—to represent Him, saying He would always be with His Church, the "gates of hell would not prevail" and the Holy Spirit would lead His Church to all Truth. The Apostles did not realize their mission would be filled with hardships and eventually martyrdom. It must have been perplexing to them to encounter hostility and rejection from some people while others accepted the word of God and His Son at the risk of their very lives. Throughout the centuries, the Gospel message has been met with love or hate, acceptance or rejection, with hearts open or closed to truth, either hardened by sin or softened by conversion and martyrdom. Yet, to this day the truth continues to be proclaimed as Jesus initially taught His Apostles.

In the mystery of God's design and great love, He does not always have a Catholic fall in love and marry another Catholic. Instead, many Catholics marry those of a different faith or someone with no faith. In these situations, the Catholic spouse must understand how they are to live their holy faith. Although the Holy Spirit converts, they are nevertheless to be the model of faith, hope and love. The Catholic spouse is commissioned in a very personal way to pray and teach through their lives of self-sacrifice, virtue, service and loving, patient explanations. St. Francis of Assisi said, "I teach the Gospel and sometimes I use words." However, some people have listened to the secular, humanist rhetoric and have abdicated their commission. We have met with couples where the Catholic says, "Oh, I'd never try to influence my spouse to become Catholic. They can do as they please." In response we ask, "When you've seen a good movie, read a good book or eaten a good meal, do you keep that to yourself and not share your wonderful new find with your beloved?" Of course, the answer is usually, "Yes, I'd share that information but not religion . . . that's personal." We continue, asking: "Jesus is far more important than food, books and movies, is He not? Isn't Jesus to be taught and shared with everyone? Religion means "relationship" between God and man. Jesus is Truth; truth is universal and must be spread. Leaving your future spouse in the dark without information that could save their soul sounds like something Satan would encourage. Wouldn't this be doing them a horrible injustice?" Sometimes these thoughts impact the couples we work with, sometimes they do not.

Satan and his minions are very busy spreading lies. We must denounce the lies and replace them with the light of truth, especially to our family. To have a truly intimate relationship with our spouse, we must stay connected in every facet of our being: mind, heart, soul, spirit, body and will. To intentionally leave one area empty is to lack true intimacy. Contrary to Cain's thinking, we are our brother's keeper but more importantly, we are our sacramental spouse's keeper! We can learn from the words of St. Ambrose who told St. Monica, when her son Augustine was a wayward pagan, to speak less to her son about God and more to God about her son! We are not to overwhelm and browbeat our spouse with information but to lovingly share our knowledge of the faith and to constantly pray and fast for them as we love them and live our faith. We are sometimes hardwired to be impatient but not having things happen quickly means we will pray longer and more fervently which just may be God's intention. Sometimes conversion happens on one's deathbed after fifty or sixty years of their Catholic spouse loving, serving, praying and fasting, trusting in total dependence on God's timing and not ours. Persistence! It is not our will but God's will we follow.

Share this with your spouse and live your *legacy of love.* As married Catholics, you are to be the example to the world of Christ's perfect, sacrificial love for His Bride, the Church. On your wedding day, you made a vow to God and your spouse to love in good times and bad, in sickness and health. Catholic marriage is not a man made contract but an unbreakable covenant between Jesus, husband and wife. Be strong in your love for God and spouse through frequent, daily prayer and living The Five Priorities each and every day. Refrain from being "of the world." Be the light and salt that Jesus has asked you to be.

Sin and More Sin

"And immediately there was in their synagogue a man with an unclean spirit; and he cried out, "What have you to do with us, Jesus of Nazareth? Have you come to destroy us? I know who you are, the Holy One of God" (Mk 1:23-24).

This is one of the many times in Scripture Jesus encountered a person possessed by an unclean spirit. As fallen, spiritual beings, they feared Him, calling Him, "The Holy One of God." Because Scripture is living and relevant, clearly warning us of Satan and his minions, we must remain vigilant of his destructive actions, especially his attempts to destroy marriage and family. Remember God's words to Cain: he could choose to be consumed by the demon or choose to be the master and turn away.

For two thousand years, the Catholic Church, faithful to the commission given by Jesus, has stood in every generation as parent and teacher, warning the faithful to be aware of Satan and his minions. She is our mother and wants to protect us. However, Satan continues to prowl about our world, always seeking to entice us to sin through thoughts like, "No one will know . . . you can handle it . . . it's really going to be a good thing . . . it's something you can't live without . . . you deserve it." In some cases, a single, solitary sin can begin a downward spiral into further sin and destruction, leading to a chaotic, dysfunctional life. Sin is destructive, leading to dangerous consequences. None of us are immune to sin and some of us may be battling more than one sin. Satan's influence is strong. He knows Scripture and he can twist it so we fail to understand the nuance of disobedience and sin. He also knows our personal weaknesses and temptations are always an attack against the weakest link of our personality. He and his minions wait with evil intent, watching like jackals hidden in the tall grass. Their seductive voices seem a part of our thoughts and are most appealing when we are at our weakest. Jesus knows we are fragile and Satan is strong and so gave us the great gift of Himself in the Sacrament of Reconciliation to help us fight temptations before they become sins. According to the Catechism of the Catholic Church (CCC 1458), the Sacrament of Reconciliation helps form our conscience, fights against evil tendencies, lets us be healed by Christ and enables us to progress in the life of the Spirit.

Jesus is the Divine Physician who loves us, knows our heart and understands our weaknesses. He offers us divine medicine in the Sacraments so we may grow in virtue and holiness and resist temptation from the enticements of sin and the oppression of demons attached to the deadly sin. After His death and resurrection, Jesus entered the locked door where the Apostles were hiding, fearing for their lives. *"Jesus said to them again, Peace be with you. As the Father has sent me, even so I send you. And when he had said this, he breathed on them and said to them, Receive the Holy Spirit. If you forgive the sins of any, they are forgiven; if you retain the sins of any, they are retained"* (Jn 20: 21-23). This breathing on the Apostles was the giving of His power and authority to breathe life into souls and restore them to their original beauty . . . only the Catholic priesthood has been vested with this power! This powerful Sacrament of Reconciliation is the medicine to cure the disease of deadly sin which makes us "soul sick." We must appreciate and use this great gift that cleans and heals the deadly wounds separating us from God. At the end of the Sacrament of Reconciliation, the priest pronounces the healing words we long for: "I absolve you from your sins, in the name of the Father, Son and Holy Spirit."

Satan, proud and disobedient, is enraged with hate at the humility required of the penitent confessing sins and asking for forgiveness. He wants to keep us bound as prisoners and slaves to deadly sin and will try to keep us from the Sacrament of Reconciliation because he knows the power of this healing Sacrament is stronger than anything he can concoct. Satan will whisper, "You're fine, you're making this little problem into a big deal. You're a good person, you haven't killed anyone. God loves you." Our conscience is designed to warn us we have sinned and the Sacrament of Reconciliation offers the opportunity to ask for forgiveness. We should be grateful for the gift of guilt that protects our soul by sending us to the Sacrament of Reconciliation. It is the built-in emergency warning system, our head and heart telling us we have offended our precious Father. We feel heart and soul sick at our bad decision. Our conscience tells us, "You made a poor decision and need to fix this now!" Jesus, in His magnanimous mercy and infinite knowledge, knows sinners sin over and over so He gave us this wonderful Sacrament to be officially and sacramentally forgiven, our sins absolved. He, the Divine Physician, puts divine, healing medicine on our souls, renewing and restoring our vital, life-giving relationship with God. Guilt is a wound begging for medical attention. It hurts and festers until it is cleaned out and healed properly. Do not listen to the seductive lies of Satan and his minions who want to weaken us and keep us in sin.

Sometimes, a Catholic priest, in being truthful, will be blunt in his counsel. Have an open heart; taking personal responsibility for our sins is facing the truth. Jesus identified Himself as Truth. Better to have a priest suggest we change specific behaviors than to carry our sins into our final meeting with Jesus. Priests have heard a million sins and have studied many years: listen to them. Some people seem to think they are doing the priest a favor by attending the Sacrament of Reconciliation. The gift of the priesthood is a gift to us from Christ. Satan is indeed very happy to have someone feel uneasy or hurt and remain upset at the priest who is helping them find a way out of their darkness. We have heard people complain that the priest in the Sacrament of Reconciliation was too tough on them and that they may well skip this Sacrament in the future. This thinking really makes little sense. We have had poor teachers but continued our education. We have had poor doctors but continued to seek medical attention. We repeat: who does not want us to have sin expunged from our soul? Who wants us to think, "I don't need reconciliation with a priest. All I need to do is tell God I'm sorry in my heart and I'm forgiven." Really? That is not what Jesus said. Do we know more than Jesus, the Divine Physician of our sick souls?

Share this with your spouse and live your *legacy of love*. We are all sinners. What sin owns you? Sins can be so ingrained that weekly reconciliation for months (or years) may be needed in an attempt to resist temptation, address the root cause, curb and eventually eliminate the sin. Finding a priest we can "connect" with will make the process easier but remember all priests have the same authority handed down through apostolic succession to grant absolution of sin. Spouses need to support each other as sin is rooted out. Seek strength through couple prayer, Mass and Eucharistic Adoration. Absolved sin may not stop the desire to flirt with sin in the future. Temptation is always the road back to sin so stay away from near occasions of temptation leading to sin. Never give up. Jesus' mercy is far greater than any sin. Our loving Father always calls us back. When a couple is dealing with several deadly sins or has been away from the Church for a long time, it is worthwhile to make the Sacrament of Reconciliation a new, weekly habit, even a date. As a couple working on holiness, attending the Sacrament of Reconciliation will give the graces needed to strengthen your souls and resolve to love God and your spouse as they deserve to be loved. Cooperate with the sacramental graces given as a great gift by focusing on prayer and sacred Scripture.

Personalities and Perceptions

VII

Personalities and Perceptions

Fake Feelings

"Now this I affirm and testify in the Lord, that you must no longer walk as the Gentiles walk, in the futility of their minds; they are darkened in their understanding, alienated from the life of God because of the ignorance that is in them, due to their hardness of heart; they have become callous and have given themselves up to licentiousness, greedy to practice every kind of uncleanness" (Eph 4:17-19).

In today's secular world, feelings have become the control center of our lives while objective truth has been forgotten. Many people live their lives on unstable, ever changing, up and down feelings. These feelings are based on a mixture of opinions, influences, ideas, positive and negative experiences that change as thinking and experiences change. This ever-changing mixture controls lives. Because feelings lack stability, lives lack stability.

Feelings, rather than truth or reality, have become the basis for many decisions. When speaking, a person will often say, "This is what I feel. You may not agree but this is how I feel." The problem is that feelings are easily distorted and often are not supported by facts or reality. However, being overwhelmed, a person may justify experiencing these feelings and cling to them. People who live their lives exclusively guided by feelings often report a lack of control—a loss of feeling grounded. They report being held captive by feelings and often confused in trying to make decisions based on feelings that may change hourly or daily.

> **All feelings are real!**
> **Not all feelings are true!**

If we believe that our feelings are real (always) and true (not always), we may base our decisions and conclusions on falsehoods. As an example, a woman who has suffered terrible abuse from a man when she is a child marries a man who loves her very much and lives his love for her every day to the best of his ability. However, regardless of his caring words and actions, she continues to "feel" unloved, certain that he could not love her, does not love her and is probably loving another, more beautiful woman, finally accusing him of infidelity. She "feels" no man is trustworthy because of her childhood experience. Their marriage is on the brink of disaster over a falsehood she believes because of her "fake feelings." As another example, a man who has been denied positive, healthy, encouraging experiences with one or both parents who then struggles with a sense of worth and value. He continues to "feel" he is a failure, unworthy of respect, struggling and failing in business and personal relationships. He "feels" unworthy of being loved and valued because of his childhood experience. In both examples, the feelings were real but not true!

We have all heard of people who seem to go through life full of negativity with a "poor me" attitude about many things. They feel blamed, unfairly treated, misunderstood, put down and have a "pity party" when life is not in a happy place. Their life is a cup "half empty." They are always upset and struggle to deal with the ups and downs of everyday situations. Frequently they say, "I just want to be happy." There are several explanations for this type of personality, ranging from genetics to early childhood and environmental traumas to painful experiences such as living with alcoholic or abusive spouses. However, the importance of family of origin cannot be overlooked. Lacking the experiences of being loved, approved of and affirmed, many children mature to adulthood with a poor sense of value or self-worth. This is most common in families suffering from the trauma of divorce. Life is a struggle to adjust to the dismantling of the family, feeling abandoned and rejected throughout their lives, especially if there has been little or no attempt on the part of the noncustodial parent to remain in their lives as a positive, encouraging, loving presence. With the dissolution of two out of every three first marriages, there are a great many children experiencing a poor sense of self-worth and a strong sense of rejection.

One of our most important responsibilities as a parent is to teach our children that happiness must be internally rather than externally centered. Happiness must come from within. We cannot depend on others to "make us happy" because that is just not possible. We will be disappointed if we depend on happiness to be supplied by another. When a person says, "I just want to be happy," they miss the point of how life works and set themselves up with unrealistic expectations. We can give ourselves an opportunity for happiness if we know we are God's beloved, a one of a kind masterpiece with a purpose and mission in life to know, love and serve Him in the life He has given us, always giving Him glory through our obedient love.

Every child needs to be told frequently until they really know deep within their soul that they are a precious, one-of-a-kind creation, gifted to their family by God with an immortal soul made in God's divine image. Children also need to hear that Jesus loves them so much because of their intrinsic value that He died for them so they can spend eternity with Him and that He has a very important plan for their lives. Finally, they need to know they were baptized into God's family and that He resides in their soul because they are His beloved, adopted child. They are loved by God and their parents. Who they are as a person is separate from what they do. They are loved because of their personhood, which is the height of God's creation. People make mistakes and poor choices; the choices they make do not mean they are a bad person.

We judge actions, not people.

We live our lives like Jesus did in obedience to the Father. Like Jesus, we want to please the Father. The Father said He was pleased with Jesus at both Jesus' baptism and at the transfiguration. We live our love for God by serving Him and the people He brings into our lives, by obeying His Commandments and Church teaching. It is the parents' responsibility to teach children that no matter what happens God does not abandon them but will always love them. They can derive peace and happiness from the certainty of His love rather than depend upon fake feelings, fun or materialism. St. Paul asks the question, *"If God is for us, who can be against us?"* (Rom 8:31b). The certitude of this knowledge can give us peace of soul no matter what we deal with in life. The love of God is real and proved by the horrible death of Jesus for each of us. We are to carry this love and peace in our hearts whether we are children, adolescents or adults; it will help all of us reject external situations threatening to destroy our peace.

Another important parental responsibility is to teach our children there are right and wrong behaviors. Two important ways of judging a course of action or making decisions: first, analyze the possible consequences of an action; then choose that option most in accord with obedience to the Ten Commandments. Many adults as well as children need to know peace is achieved through obedience and not simply doing what they feel like doing: "I want to do this and I feel I can do this; it's okay for me to be unfaithful, as this person makes me feel happy; I feel God is telling me I can do what I want for my own happiness; God won't mind, I'm a good person." This thinking is from Satan who wants to trick us into disobedience. Peace of mind, peace of soul and true happiness only come from living our love for God through obedience to Jesus and His Church.

Obedience brings peace.

Feelings have become the focus of decision-making, resulting in terrible life decisions because they are ever-changing, unreliable and often shortsighted. We feel loved or unloved, happy or unhappy all within a day, causing havoc to personal relationships and family life. Who wants to throw us off balance, have us feel unloved, discouraged and filled with worry? Satan, of course, who tempts us with negative feelings of discouragement, anger, depression or abandonment. We must guard our thoughts and feelings; dealing with Satan is part of life.

The Church on earth is called the Church Militant because we are in a constant battle against the world, the flesh and the devil. We must arm ourselves with prayer and the Sacraments, the weapons Jesus gave us to use as a means of protection, strength and growth. Turn to God in total surrender knowing even in the darkest hour, He is there even though we may feel alone.

Share this with your spouse and live your *legacy of love*. Help each other discern the facts of truth from the fiction of feelings. Jesus identified himself as the Truth. If you remain rooted in Jesus . . . the Truth . . . you can discern truth from fiction. When you feel unloved, remember the truth is God loves you, Jesus died for you and you have a special purpose that only you can accomplish. When making a decision, ask if it conforms to God's will found in the teachings of His Church and the Commandments. Help each other remain grounded in the truth of Christ and His Church. Guard your feelings and know Jesus is with you even in your darkest hour. Turn to Him with the Chaplet of Divine Mercy.

Walk with Him through the Stations of the Cross. Pray the rosary. All prayer will strengthen you, calm you and give you peace. Never take prayer out of your life; it is a true lifeline to the heart of Jesus.

Anger

*"Sin is lurking at the door; its desire is for you,
but you must master it"* (Gen. 4:7b).

God warned Cain that his anger was like a controlling demon. Sadly, he ignored God and killed his brother.

Anger is one of the Seven Deadly Sins resulting in a loss of emotional control. It is a sin against the gift of love. Some people justify their anger, saying, "Jesus got angry at the moneychangers in the temple, so it's okay for me to get angry and lose it." No, it is not. When Jesus drove the moneychangers out of the Temple, He was fulfilling prophetic Scripture, cleansing the temple in His zeal for His Father's house. We would do well to remember Jesus is God; we are not. He has perfect love; we do not. In the depths of His agony while hanging on the cross, He forgave His executioners and never uttered a word of anger. Tempted by Satan, He retained His emotional control.

Anger, as an uncontrolled way of life is a serious issue, an ongoing, deeply felt emotion of living, thinking and feeling. It is always present. Although either or both spouses may struggle with anger, often it is husbands that are caught in this deadly emotion. Anger attacks and inflicts destructive outbursts of pain and is always demeaning and controlling. Wives feel worthless, wanting so often to give up, expressing fear for themselves and for the well-being of their children, who often experience a growing fear of their father and depreciating treatment toward them.

One source of anger dates back thirty-thousand years: the combination of testosterone, muscle mass and strength that enabled our male ancestors to protect and defend their family from attacking groups and destructive forces. This combination aided families to survive horrible events in cultures without military or law enforcement. The husband and oldest sons put themselves between danger and the mother and younger children, fighting to the death with their physical strength and prowess. However, we now live in a world that no longer needs men to wrestle marauders or wild animals for protection or food. Today, many men have sedentary jobs. While working in an office may bring its own set of stressors, most men have few opportunities to address stress and the resulting frustration and anger in an appropriate manner. This can lead to a breaking point where the slightest disturbance or drive home in traffic becomes the fuse to set off an explosion. That explosion reaches full force as they return home after a long, stressful, frustrating and perhaps nonproductive day, walking through the door and directing their anger toward wife and children. The irony is that the gift of strength and testosterone given to a man to protect his family from danger is now unleashed on those he loves. Instead of protecting the family, his anger is used to destroy them. Such a man needs consistent physical exercise to clear the mind of stress and allow his testosterone levels to decrease. It is hard for so many men to find time to exercise because of long work hours and the responsibilities of a family. However, developing a physical exercise program, although a small step, is an important one.

A second source of anger is that of learned behavior from our family of origin. Families imprint our future behaviors. An angry father will be remembered with fear and possibly hatred. Often children will repeat what they learned from him during childhood, even though they hated this aspect of their family life. If it is learned behavior and repeated, it will become generational sin passed down from grandfather to father to son. On a positive note: while family of origin influences who we are, our work, effort and determination influence who we become.

Finally, and perhaps the most powerful and insidious of all sources of anger is that it is one of the Seven Deadly Sins. It is a spiritual cancer of the head and heart. It is used by Satan who lays in wait for the next issue to present itself, using it to trigger a massive meltdown, resulting in seething, all-consuming anger, the lurking demon seeking to control us and become our master as it became Cain's master. It is truly disturbing to think we are in the grip of one of Satan's minions. How does one deal with a demon? Spiritual warfare requires spiritual weapons. Jesus in His total and everlasting mercy gave His Church antidotes to the deadly poison of sin, especially deadly sin. In His breathing on His Apostles and in His words, He conferred on them the power of the Sacrament of Reconciliation: *"Receive the Holy Spirit. If you forgive the sins of any, they are forgiven; if you retain the sins of any, they are retained"* (Jn 20:22b, 23). Jesus is waiting to begin the process of removing the demon of anger from our lives. However, it will be a process. Deadly sin can oppress us, wreaking havoc in our lives and injuring our loved ones. Once the sin of anger is ingrained, it is very hard to expiate. It may have been with us for years and so it may take years to subdue and overcome. Ridding ourselves of a serious, destructive sin takes time, perseverance and determination. It does not matter how long it takes but it does matter that we care enough about our families to stop destroying them. Expiating serious sin is a long journey. We can begin today by apologizing to our family for all the painful situations we have put them through. We can listen with humble patience to some of the hurts they have been carrying in their broken hearts. They will say, "Remember the time you said or did. . . ." and we can answer, "I am so very sorry for the pain I have caused you. Please forgive me." It is also important for us to attend the weekly Sacrament of Reconciliation and ask Jesus for the virtue of self-control as well as to forgive the pain caused to our family. Keeping a journal of all the times we experience anger and taking the journal with us where we can explain the situations, triggers and angry responses can also be a great help as it allows for honest confessing. It will take time but eventually the lurking demon can be subdued. Do not give up! Relapses will occur as we are not perfect. This deadly sin may have been with us for decades. Satan does not want to let any of us go. However, we can use our free will, the love of our family and sacramental grace to expel him.

We should be in control of ourselves rather than relinquish our God-given free will to Satan, who wants to destroy us and our marriage, family and children. We should be determined to make sure this terrible behavior does not continue into future generations with our sons repeating the patterns of anger and our daughters seeking angry men for marriage. All of us as husbands, wives and parents are in a spiritual battle. We must persevere and win the battle for our soul and the souls of our spouse and children. Finally, please remember the father of the home represents God the Father. He is strong, powerful, makes the rules and is bigger than life to his little children. However, if this bigger-than-life person represents a God who is angry, unforgiving and mean-spirited, his children may well become anti-Catholic and atheistic. They may well hate the "god" of their home and childhood.

Catholic therapy can explore the reasons for anger. Individuals and families can learn what to do when a trigger is tripped; they can develop strategies and tools to deal with the anger and gain understanding to facilitate changes in thinking and behaving. But, only Jesus can give us strength and the needed graces to combat Satan and sin. Only Jesus' sacramental grace has the power to heal the soul from deadly sin with the medicine obtained in the Sacrament of Reconciliation.

Once our spiritual armor is in place, we can then use these additional approaches to managing anger:

Focus on situations and factors that trigger angry responses.

What causes the angry behavior? Feeling criticized, condemned, rejected or controlled can lead to explosive behaviors. Thinking influences feelings. Are there specific, automatic, hostile thoughts about a situation or encounter with another that trigger the angry feelings? As an example, when we think our spouse is not listening to what we are saying, we may automatically begin to feel ignored, hurt or angry. Telling our spouse that we know they are busy but letting them know that setting aside time to listen to our frustrations and stressors of the day is usually helpful. Negative thoughts can also be addressed by shifting from negative to realistic thinking, examining other options such as, "Well, maybe my spouse is also feeling stressed and overwhelmed by the day and still has a lot of stuff that needs to be done." Examining thoughts that lead to angry feelings can help prevent sliding into angry responses. Understanding and sympathizing with the pressures and demands of our beloved can help us leave our own angry thinking and shift gears from an angry to a helpful spouse.

Share this with your spouse and live your *legacy of love*. If you have made your spouse or children the brunt of your anger, make use of the tools Jesus provides in the Sacraments, apologize and attend the Sacrament of Reconciliation. Do not put off the divine medicine as Satan will do everything to discourage you. Do not let him win!

Bite Your Tongue

"But no human being can tame the tongue—a restless evil,
full of deadly poison. With it we bless the Lord and Father,
and with it we curse men, who are made in the likeness of God.
From the same mouth come blessing and cursing" (Jas 3:8-10).

Husbands and wives have said terrible, hurtful things when embroiled in an argument. We have said it, we cannot take it back and we feel really bad about it. Speaking in anger, frustration or simply without thinking of the impact of our words, we have caused hurt between our spouse, ourselves and our marriage. Even after there has been forgiveness, the words can remain as an indelible mark on our beloved's heart. Words have weight and consequences whether they are intentional or unintentional.

> **WORDS ARE IMPORTANT.**
> **God created everything through the power of His Word.**
> **Jesus is the Eternal Word made Flesh.**
> **Scripture is the life-giving Word of God.**

There is concern today about the younger generation not taking personal responsibility. The seeds of their poor behavior can often be traced to their family of origin where parents said terrible things to each other without apologizing. They showed no true sorrow for their angry outbursts, repeating their poor behavior over and over, inflicting angry words, refusing to apologize, admit wrongdoing or accept personal responsibility for their words and actions. They pretended nothing happened, continuing their daily conversations, completely ignoring the pain and hurt inflicted on their beloved spouse and family.

Self-control is needed to cease using angry words to injure others without regard for the pain that is caused. Between the feeling of anger and the barrage of angry words that follow, we must develop self-control. It is not easy to stop once anger takes hold of us. It is similar to speeding and needing to stop before hitting another car. After impact, saying "sorry" or pretending it never happened will not work out well. It will also not work out well if we injure our beloved and pretend all is "okay." The next time anger, impatience or frustration is about to take hold, jam on the "emotional" and "verbal" brakes to avoid injuries. It is easier to deal with one problem versus several. When busy and suddenly faced with an issue that needs immediate attention, we can become frustrated and impatient or we can choose to stop, take a deep breath and deal with it kindly rather than explode by saying terrible things to those we love. When this happens, we have multiplied one problem into three: the original issue, an injured spouse and a damaged relationship.

Even though we sweep outbursts of cruel, angry words under the carpet, they will be imprinted into the memories of our loved ones who continue to endure hurt and pain caused by an uncontrolled temper. Week after week, month after month, year after year, the scars mount until the recipient of the anger is finally done and files for divorce or the vulnerable, brokenhearted spouse falls into the arms of someone else who will give them love, encouragement and affirmation. The offending spouse is shocked and says, "I don't know what happened. Why did my spouse do that? I've always been so faithful." Really? Fidelity is about far more than being in a relationship with someone other than one's spouse. It is about being faithful to one's wedding vows to love and honor in good times and bad, in sickness and health, until parted by death. Angry, terrible words are not loving or honorable.

> We have chosen hateful words over loving our spouse.
>
> We have chosen to dishonor our beloved spouse through words and action.

Personal change is difficult because we defend, deflect and deny anything we perceive as a weakness or impediment in our personality. If it is ONE spouse's problem, then it is BOTH spouses' problem! This is a sacramental marriage in which all is shared . . . even the problems. We are each responsible to help our spouse reach heaven. When communication is an issue, please listen and learn from what your spouse says they need. Turn down the volume of your voice and address the tone: a loud voice that is strong and used to gain control is aggressive; a dictatorial tone is demeaning and preachy. No one wants to be spoken to in this way. If our spouse asks for a lower voice and kinder tone, it will benefit us to listen and fix it . . . fast! The fallout from failing to address this issue may be that our spouse will stop speaking and listening to us. They may just check out of the relationship for self-preservation.

As Catholics, we are taught in second grade the wonderful, healing power of the Sacrament of Reconciliation in which we humbly apologize to Jesus through the office of the priesthood. We replace the pride of having committed sins that offend God with true, humble repentance for our transgressions, allowing us to be open to God's abundant graces. We must possess a willing spirit, open heart and sincerity of determination for change. Exerting self-control over our fallen nature requires spiritual strength from prayer as well as fidelity to the Sacraments.

As we have said, keeping a written log listing the number of times anger was expressed or felt like being expressed is important. Why? For three reasons:

We become more aware of our anger and more serious about rooting out this deadly sin.

The priest understands how this deadly sin has affected our life.

Satan is put on notice that we are determined to eradicate our sin of anger.

We must always remember that words have the power to build up or tear down and destroy. Not only does anger and angry words kill our soul but they destroy those around us, the very people God gave us to love and nurture. St. Ignatius of Loyola's prayer "Anima Christi" identifies Satan as the "malignant enemy." When we have been wounded, our fallen nature leads us to wound others. One wound causes another, the malignancy grows and is passed on to others.

The injured spouse will eventually need to clean out all the wounds from the hurtful words, actions and tone that have been buried deep within their heart, mind and soul for so long. Even though they are a victim, years of pain surge to the surface, exploding in anger they were never allowed to express as they kept the temperament of the home calm so their angry spouse would not erupt again and again. Now, they cannot forgive their spouse for the pain they have endured. The malignant enemy has succeeded in transferring the sin to the victim and now both spouses lack a clean heart. For both husband and wife, it becomes necessary to avail themselves of the great gift of Jesus awaiting in the Sacrament of Reconciliation to heal each of them with His divine medicine and graces.

St. James says the tongue is a fire from hell that cannot be tamed. When we allow Satan to control our thoughts, we will have no opportunity to tame that fire. Thoughts can easily turn mean, angry and hurtful, finally erupting through our tongue. Do not be duped by Satan: stop the angry thoughts so the words will not follow.

During the Catholic Mass, we make the sign of the cross on our forehead, lips and heart just prior to the proclaiming of the Holy Gospel. As we trace the cross on these three areas, we say to ourselves, "May the Lord be in my mind, on my lips and in my heart." Please, repeat this beautiful prayer frequently every day to tame wayward tongues into submission. With our mind, lips and heart working together, we can, with God's help, use our tongues properly.

Share this with your spouse and live your *legacy of love*. Developing self-control is a process and all processes take time, usually months rather than a few days or weeks. Persevere! Develop a game plan and make it your focus. When a situation or trigger infuriates you: STOP, BREATHE, ASK JESUS TO HELP YOU and be SILENT! Satan's scheme is to take control of the situation; he wants to destroy the marriage by inflicting pain on your heart and your spouse's heart. He is a master at duping you into exploding with a barrage of angry words and demeaning your spouse with volume or tone. Be strong: do not injure your sacramental marriage, your family and your future generations. Slow down, refocus on personal prayer and ask for the strength to disengage rather than injure your beloved.

Patience or Impatience?

"Love is patient and kind; love is not jealous or boastful; it is not arrogant or rude. Love does not insist on its own way; it is not irritable or resentful; it does not rejoice at wrong, but rejoices in the right. Love, bears all things, believes all things, hopes all things, endures all things"
(Cor 13:4-7).

This is a favorite reading chosen by couples on their wedding day focusing on selflessness and the virtue of humility. The person in love lives their love in very real and tangible ways, placing their beloved's needs before their own. Rather than taking control and making decisions based on what they want or need, they first consider the wants and needs of their spouse. They consult with their spouse, seeking to understand their thoughts and making decisions as a couple. They practice listening before speaking, knowing the importance of understanding and appreciating. A key asset is the humble approach of patience. Humble Jesus came to serve. Proud Satan refused to serve; his singular ambition was to control mankind by coaxing, tempting and tricking each of us to turn from God to sin.

As followers of Jesus, we are to conform our will to His. We emulate Him, wanting to please our Father as He did. However, the truth is that this beautiful passage in Corinthians takes a lifetime of hard work to achieve. It becomes even more difficult if we lack patience. When we add to our fallen nature the personal experiences of observing and experiencing firsthand our parents' lack of patience, we understand how difficult it is to develop this virtue. Patience is complex, requiring us to exercise self-control of behavior, words and attitudes in situations that are emotionally charged. Kindness follows patience, asking for gentleness and sweet behavior in dealing with our spouse as opposed to blaming, controlling with cross words, depreciating tones, name-calling or other displays of anger.

When we truly understand the sacramental nature of marriage and choose to live our love for our spouse daily, we will develop and practice patience and kindness, treating them with respect, attention and encouragement. We will train ourselves to calmly deal with frustration in a way that words and tone are controlled, calmly explaining our thoughts, needs or areas of frustration. Words are expressed in a way that is not condescending, rude or angry. Kind and direct communication allows our spouse to listen and understand what we are saying and need. When things go wrong, we do not blame our spouse but focus on an attitude of peace.

Learning patience and achieving a measure of peace in our non-peaceful world becomes easier if we accept God's timing and plan may not be ours. He is in control. We are to do our best in the tasks we are given, exercising our free will and determination to work His plan and submitting our will to Him: "Okay God, what's going on right at this moment? What do we need to do now? Please help us." We can do our best, work so hard and yet have it all fall apart. It is at times like these we must remain focused on the "big picture" remembering God is with us. He is always shaping us into a deeper relationship with Him, desiring us to rely on Him, trust Him and to know He loves us and will never abandon us. However, this does not mean He will not present us with challenging, sometimes very difficult situations to learn to accept and work within His holy will.

Satan wants us to misuse the gifts God has given us. When time is tight or things have gone wrong, he promotes unhealthy behaviors by cajoling us to become frustrated and impatient with our spouse and children. Then we explode with anger, harsh words and rude behavior, displaying impatience and a lack of respect to those we most love. Habits are hard to shed. They may eventually become destructive patterns of behavior with hooks that dig deep into our personality and souls, injuring spouse and family. They are spiritual illnesses in need of spiritual medicine. These hooks are difficult to eliminate because they are deeply imbedded. Satan wants to control us with unhealthy, toxic behavior patterns and addictions. Impatience can lead to angry outbursts but also the desire to control as Satan controls when we give in to impatient and sinful behavior. We become determined, thinking, "I'm going to be in control here. It's going to be my way!" This leads to the deadly sin of pride. We begin to think we are a god, wanting our own way and insisting everyone do as we say. God gifts us with freedom but Satan seeks to steal our freedom by enslaving and controlling us. We are patient with ourselves but not with God or spouse. We are kind to ourselves but not to spouse or family.

> **Control is only to be used on one's self;
> that is the virtue of self-discipline.**
>
> **Control is not to be used on others;
> that is following Satan, not God.**

Frequently, both spouses vie for control, making use of anger, harsh tones, intimidation, unkind words, tears, threats and manipulation. This is not patience, love or kindness. Many couples never alter this toxic lifestyle and those around them feel very uncomfortable listening to this ongoing, negative communication.

Self-seeking relationships are based on a "me first, my way is better, my way or the highway" attitude. Thinking of self before spouse is not love. Behaving as if the universe revolves around us is not selfless, loving, patient or kind. A stubborn, unbending personality is very difficult to live with. However, the good news is that we are capable of change if we choose to use our free will by practicing patience and remain determined to change our unhealthy behaviors, reminding ourselves we are not God and remember He does have a plan for all of us if we will only cooperate.

To repeat: negative behaviors are spiritual sicknesses and need spiritual medicine found in the Sacrament of Reconciliation. If these behaviors are ingrained in our personalities, then we must attend to the Sacrament of Reconciliation every time they manifest themselves. The power of Jesus and our openhearted willingness to change can help us grow as Catholic spouses. We can develop a willingness to please our spouse, listening to them and considering their thoughts and feelings before our own. We can receive strength and graces through the Sacraments, enabling us to become more flexible and willing to place our spouse first.

Sometimes, a lack of patience may stem from a superior attitude, thinking we are better than our spouse. Depreciation of spouse then easily follows. We may think our family of origin is better, smarter or possesses more education and conclude these things make us superior to our spouse. However, these are not important criteria to God. God loves our spouse as much as He loves us.

> **God is more pleased with humble behavior than arrogant pride.**

Angry personalities are not the best candidates for marriage. Such individuals are easily provoked and may often use anger to control spouse and family. Everyone walks on eggshells trying to keep peace at any price. The angry, controlling spouse may blame their manipulative vice on just needing to "let off steam." However, if they do not blow up at friends or colleagues at work, then fits of anger are usually a means of control used to get one's way at home much as a spoiled child throwing a tantrum.

To those who are engaged to a future spouse lacking in patience and using anger to control or depreciate, perhaps rethinking the relationship is in order; such behavior may only increase after marriage. If your future spouse says their anger is because they are being provoked, there is a good chance they are not taking personal responsibility for their behavior. Do not be blamed for their wrongdoing; seek counseling from a priest or Catholic therapist.

If married to an angry, controlling or inflexible person, the first question to ask is whether you are in a dangerous situation. If you are in a situation that is abusive and living with a spouse who struggles with self-control, then seek the aid of family, friends, pastor or the authorities rather than remain in a potentially dangerous situation. It is unlawful to be struck, knocked or pinned down, locked in a room or put into any dangerous situation. Understand though, these situations are different from disagreements or simple arguments devoid of aggression where no one is injured physically or emotionally. Misunderstandings and disagreements are not abuse; they occur in every marriage. It is important to isolate these disagreements and work through them rather than sharing such incidents with family or friends who may misunderstand, thereby causing a breakdown of relationships or division with in-laws.

Love desires the best for one's beloved.

Love brings us closer to God.

Love does not take advantage.

Love places the beloved's best interest
before one's self-gratification.

Love is absent of fear and intimidation.

Just as Christ lived His love for us by sacrificing Himself for His Bride, the Church, there are times we are to sacrifice for our spouse. Love is a decision to remain committed and devoted to one another. Constantly striving to practice the kind of love St. Paul speaks of in his letter to the Corinthians is a lifelong, humbling endeavor. What is important is that we never give up but continue to ask Jesus to forgive our impatience and increase our capacity to love our spouse as we vowed on our wedding day. When we think we cannot love our spouse anymore, we look at the crucifix and return to the Sacrament of Reconciliation to ask Jesus to increase our capacity to love.

Share this with your spouse and live your *legacy of love*. Did you choose this passage of St. Paul's letter to the Corinthians for your wedding? On a scale of one to ten, what is your level of patience? Do not become discouraged if you have trouble learning patience and kindness. Keep trying: work daily on developing and practicing patience versus seeking to control. Speak with kindness and respect, always be willing to listen (listening is not necessarily agreement) and work toward joint decision-making versus manipulating to "get" your way through controlling emotions such as anger. Kind conversations between spouses, free to express their true feelings, is a big step toward patience. Ask your spouse if they feel they walk on eggshells or if they are at times fearful. If they are, take their comments as acknowledgments and do not get angry. Just know that you have work to do. Ask your spouse for help and work together to achieve true love. Thank God every day for His patience to all of us who fall so short of the ideal of obedient love.

A Little Bit of Poison

"A new commandment I give to you, that you love one another; even as I have loved you, that you also love one another. By this all men will know that you are my disciples, if you have love for one another" (Jn 13:34).

Jesus lived His love for humanity by serving, ultimately sacrificing His life for His Bride, the Church. Of His own free will, He died a horrific death out of obedient love for His Father and merciful love for humanity. We are to do as He did by serving and sacrificing for our spouse and children, always willing to die to our selfish pride. However, self-sacrifice is based on self-discipline and our fallen nature has hardwired us to be self-centered. God desires us to use our free will for obedient love while Satan desires us to remain lazy and self-centered, discouraging any attempt at self-discipline. Determination and the frequent use of sacramental grace can lead us to self-discipline. Making use of a specific virtue to counteract the vice that seeks to control us is always helpful and the direction of a spiritual advisor is essential. As we grow closer to God in virtue, we become an easier person to live with and our home and family life become more peaceful. What is the prime ingredient for us to desire this kind of revolutionary change in our character? It is the willingness to positively use our FREE WILL!

That is the good news! Now . . . the bad news: many people do not want to use their free will to develop self-discipline but choose to misuse the gift of free will by willfully living their life focused on individual, selfish interests, basing decisions on what they want or need, irrespective of the wants or needs of their spouse or family. This selfish attitude is poison. When we are so consumed with thoughts of ourselves, we have no time to love God, spouse or children.

> **Christ is ever-present in our sacramental marriage! We are to dedicate our lives to making it the best it can be!**

Catholic marriage is a covenant, our vocation and our Sacrament. We are to dedicate our lives to making it the best it can possibly be!

Do these concepts seem lofty or ethereal? Take a minute . . . and a few deep breaths. Imagine you are co-piloting a plane with your spouse and family onboard. You would never dream of ignoring the safety rules as that would endanger the lives of your family. Neither spouse would intentionally crash the plane. However, this is exactly what a self-centered spouse does. They reason, "I work hard, now I just want to have fun. I want to be happy. I deserve to be happy. I must look out for myself so I can have fun. I have needs and I will fill my needs as I see fit." They do not ask what their spouse wants or needs. Everything is about "Me, Me, Me." Decisions are based on their needs, likes, dislikes and interests. Spouse and family quickly learn they are along only for the ride. A selfish spouse cannot be depended upon. They will be a part of the family when it works for them but if plans change they will do what most suits them. Family outings, children's sports, any number of events may be planned on and even reminded through texts or notes but attendance will remain questionable. The truly sad part is that events are rarely attended by the selfish spouse, not because of business or personal emergencies but because other events are more interesting or exciting.

The message is communicated loud and clear that what their spouse and family think, say or do has little or no value to them. A spouse's selfish behavior injected into family life is like ingesting a little bit of poison every day, slowly sickening family life and love.

Are we selfish? How would our spouse answer this question? When we are asked to do something, do we show displeasure by acting irritable, grumpy, withholding love, complaining or depreciating spouse and family because we do not want to be bothered? Do we ignore what our spouse asks of us? Are work, electronics, sports and friends more important than family? Answering "yes" to any of these questions should lead us to rethink the gift of free will given specifically for the purpose of living Christ's love. If God called us home right now, how would our soul look to Him? Would God say, *"Well done, good and faithful servant; you have been faithful over a little, I will set you over much; enter into the joy of your master"* (Mt 25:21) or would He have another message for us?

Share this with your spouse and live your *legacy of love.* First of all, acknowledge and own selfish behavior. Satan desires you deny your self-centered, selfish actions and to fail at any attempt to change vices into virtues. Do the opposite: select one behavior to change and work on it daily, sending the message to spouse and family your desire to become the spouse and parent they deserve. Secondly, tell your spouse and family how much you love them and apologize for previous behaviors that were hurtful. Each day, put spouse and family first, finding out what they want or need. Third, learn more about your beloved spouse and family. Ask questions, listen, learn what is important to them as well as their likes and dislikes. Fourth, turn to Jesus in the Sacrament of Reconciliation and receive His gift of undying love, understanding and mercy. He is the Divine Physician and His gift of sacramental grace is available to all of us as medicine for our soul to eradicate the poison of selfishness.

The Speck and the Stick

"Why do you see the speck that is in your brother's eye,
but do not notice the log that is in your own eye? Or how can you say
to your brother, "Let me take the speck out of your eye, when there is
the log in your own eye? You hypocrite, first you take the log out of
your own eye, and then you will see clearly to take the speck out of
your brother's eye" (Mt 7:3-5).

Scripture is clear about judging others, admonishing us lest we be judged. Unfortunately, the person we often judge most harshly is our spouse. That wonderful person we could not wait to marry has turned out to have flaws! We have spoken to them about their flaws and still they continue to repeat the same behaviors over and over! We have tried to fix the situation through nagging, controlling or withholding affection but have been unsuccessful. We know we are right and they are wrong. We feel quite justified that we have healthy behaviors while they have very unhealthy behaviors. We may very well punish our spouse for years and feel extremely justified in doing so.

Do we misjudge our spouse frequently or do we give them the benefit of the doubt? When we meet Jesus, we do not want to hear Him say it was our eye that had the plank and our spouse's eye with the tiny speck. We may even be the cause of our spouse's speck of imperfection. When we are about to complain and crit-icize our spouse, we begin with the false disclaimer, "Of course I'm not perfect, BUT . . . ." then speak of our spouse's sins and infractions to justify, "I'm okay, you're not, you own the problem." Our spouse then remains the sole owner of the problem. We are correct in saying we are not perfect but we need to focus on our imperfections rather than those of our spouse.

Each of us is imperfect. Complaining about our spouse instead of working on our own personality flaws is hypocritical. When we do so, we are engaging in the sin of pride. Remember, pride was Satan's sin in his belief he was equal to God. Only God is perfect and able to judge. Only He is both just and merciful. Being neither, we ought to leave judgement to God and work on our own flaws. One day each of us will stand alone before the throne of God. We will not be able to make excuses or hide behind our spouse saying it is their fault and not ours. We will stand alone. Now that is a sobering image!

> **If we want to change our marriage or our spouse, we must first change ourselves!**

Science tells us for every action there is a reaction. As we change our behavior, our spouse's behavior will also change. What is important is to focus on control of self rather than control of spouse. Rather than nagging, let us focus on appropriate actions, including ongoing behaviors of respect and affection so as not to deprive each other from the love both need and want.

As a Sacrament of the Catholic Church, we are bound to our spouse for life. Learning self-discipline and changing ourselves to be more loving and accepting of our spouse and their flaws is for our own spiritual growth but understand, it takes a lifetime of ups and downs to accomplish. We are commissioned to grow in love and obedience to God by changing those negative aspects of our personality to have a healthier, happier, holier Catholic marriage. However, we cannot change ourselves nor influence our spouse toward change solely through human actions, so we turn to merciful Jesus for help. We love our spouse. We devote ourselves to them, serving and sacrificing for them. We must not believe we have the answers or presume we are always right and our spouse is always wrong. We must not leave as Judas did.

Instead, we must turn to Jesus in prayer and the Sacraments, especially in the Sacrament of Reconciliation, begging Him to forgive our pride and to increase our capacity to love. We are in a spiritual battle; Jesus gave us the weapons to win this battle by working on personal holiness and learning to love as He taught us to love.

Annoying habits and strong personality defects can be very irritating to live with every day. However, if our response is consistently rude or angry, then the wedge driven between us and our spouse will become an even bigger chasm. Instead of trying to change our spouse, we need to change our response to them. When our spouse says "A" which makes us crazy and our response is always "B" which makes our spouse angry, stop replying with the same response. Instead, say something sweet or nothing at all. Turn a negative into a positive and grow in holiness by speaking positively or not at all!

There is a story we heard about a very devout and prayerful Catholic couple. After a decade of marriage, the husband developed a heart condition that would not allow him to work. The stay-at-home wife went to work to support him and their child, accepting this new challenge in her life as God's will. She did well in the corporate world and moved from secretary to executive in a few short years. He was proud of her accomplishments but very resentful of his loss of health and earning power. He felt demeaned in being the stay-at-home dad. His wife would come home from the office, kick off her shoes by the front door, drop her briefcase, throw her jacket on a chair and leave clothes all over the bedroom as she put on her robe. He asked her over and over to pick up after herself, eventually becoming angry, telling her she was disrespecting him. She would say she was sorry but it never changed. One day, he read a book about St. Therese of Lisieux explaining how she offered every pain, problem and task, regardless of the level of difficulty, to God. The husband decided to pick everything up without anger, offering all to Jesus for the graces he needed to accept his life. He began to greet his tired wife at the door with a smile, picking everything up without complaining. He complained about nothing and was determined to be a really pleasant, happy guy. This went on for a few weeks. His wife began to realize his changed behavior and asked him why. When he told her, she looked at him and said, "Wow, my messiness has become a cause of grace for you? I'm going to start picking up my own stuff so I can have grace too!"

How pleased God must be when we take a negative and turn it into a positive! This couple took the plank in one eye and the stick in the other and turned them both into grace, changing their behaviors of judging, complaining and refusing to listen or change. Offering suffering, no matter how large or small, is a peaceful acceptance of God's Holy Will, at the same time allowing us to address our selfish, self-centered, fallen nature toward our beloved spouse. We can all adopt this holy habit of ceasing to judge and complain and instead change our behaviors, offering them as holy sacrifices to God.

Share this with your spouse and live your *legacy of love*. Each couple is aware of annoying or unhealthy habits their beloved would like to see changed. Make no excuses. Take on the challenge of changing unkind, unloving, disrespectful or personally unhealthy behaviors as a gift of love from you to God and to your spouse. Habits are difficult to break, especially if they are sinful. Satan wants to chain you down, control and enslave you while Jesus desires you to be free. The Sacrament of Reconciliation will assist you when you are tempted or fall prey to sinful habits. Deeply ingrained sins need to be dealt with very strongly as spiritual attacks. Satan hates the Sacrament of Reconciliation: it is a Sacrament of humility and a powerful spiritual counterattack to sin, giving the penitent strength and grace. It may take months to replace an unhealthy habit with a healthy one. Going from vice to virtue will be a battle but with sacramental grace, wars are won. Stay the course! Do not give up! Recite the Chaplet of Divine Mercy as part of the healthy, new habit. Ask Jesus for His help to be kind to your spouse and to increase your capacity to love. Keep cleaning house on unhealthy habits!

Stuck in Arguing

"I therefore, a prisoner for the Lord, beg you to walk in a manner worthy of the calling to which you have been called, with all lowliness and meekness, with patience, forbearing one another in love, eager to maintain the unity of the Spirit in the bond of peace" (Eph 4:1-3).

Some couples spend their entire married life arguing with one another. They argue over anything and everything with life becoming one long debate. It is exhausting being in the presence of such people. Each proud spouse holds tightly to their opinions, ideas and perspective, certain they are right and just as certain their spouse is wrong. They are competitors in a continuous battle of wills. "My will over yours!" becomes the battle cry as each try to control the other. They are stuck, locked into their own personalities much like wild animals who fight to their own demise. Unfortunately, they never reach a solution, never resolve anything. The more they argue, the more stuck they become.

Catholic marriage is not a competition or a battle of wills. It is not a game of winners and losers. It is accepting one's spouse as a great gift from God. What kind of marriage does God desire? One of love, peace, support, patience, forgiveness, humility, self-denial and the willingness to serve one's beloved. In marriage, we are to be helpmates to our spouse, offering our talents to share and learn from each other. Unwillingness to learn from one's spouse, arguing over every decision and idea one's beloved suggests is true ignorance.

Years ago, we experienced an evening of endurance in accepting an invitation to dinner with another couple. Gary and I had no idea how they treated each other. When she was telling a story, saying it happened on Tuesday, he interrupted and corrected her saying, "No, no, no. It was Wednesday not Tuesday." When he began to share, she corrected and clarified nearly all his thoughts. They spent much of dinner criticizing and complaining about each other This was the pattern of the evening; we left exhausted!

> **Marriage is not about WHO is right but WHAT is right.**
>
> **God, His perfect love and His perfect will is what is right.**

Scripture is filled with proud, tragic personalities who thought they were right. The learned scribes and Pharisees thought they knew God's plan about the promised Messiah. Not only did they not recognize Jesus but killed Him as a dangerous imposter. The willful and proud prodigal son turned his back on the loving will of his father, demanding his inheritance and behaving as if his only tie to his father was money. The "bad" thief on the cross chided and denounced Jesus in His agony, refusing to believe He was truly God.

Stubborn, stuck personalities have a hard time learning and changing. They believe they are the smartest person in the room. Blinded by pride, they refuse help, change or growth, clinging to the attitude of, "This is who I am. I am always right." They remind us of the animals stuck, mired down in the tar pits who after using all their strength to free themselves, eventually died. Argumentative people are much the same way. Some couples view a difference of opinion as an opportunity to interrogate, debate and argue, much as a prosecuting attorney focused on the single-minded goal to win their case. Such ongoing, intense drama can destroy a sacramental marriage, causing a spouse to lose heart and simply give up. Argumentative people are the real losers in these situations because everyone just stops talking to them.

Husbands and wives: make a vow to love and honor each other. Arguing is not loving or honorable. When we engage in this type of behavior, we are breaking our marriage vows and being unfaithful to our spouse! When we return home at the end of the day, we are to help create an environment of love. Why? Because we are the school of love to our family and that is the role God expects from us, His adopted children.

When returning home at the end of the day, mentally shift gears. Try to leave the stressors of the day behind. Think, "I will make a conscious decision not to argue with my spouse. I will not stress over the little stuff. I will enjoy my spouse and my family. They are not the enemy." Remind yourself that you are about to reconnect with your most precious gifts from God. Hugs, kisses and maybe just listen. Enjoy the chaos of your family! Ask what you can do to assist. Listen to what needs to be done and dive in, ready to change diapers, assist with homework, help with dinner or run a last-minute errand. Be a lifesaver and hero. This is how to teach the next generation how to live as a Catholic family.

When conflict arises, begin by offering to assist in fixing the problem in an impartial, objective manner, without blame, criticism or rebuke. Be willing to accept some of the responsibility for the conflict, especially if it is applicable. Adding divisive blame to the original issue only escalates conflict, doubling it in scope. Instead of lashing out, driving a wedge between the two of you, reach out in loving support and work together to solve the issue with kindness, respect and patience. Address the conflict or issue as a problem to be solved rather than as an opportunity to blame or enhance your own sense of superiority.

Share this with your spouse and live your *legacy of love*. Arguing and being stuck in a negative personality is a recipe for heartache. Be the leader that changes the environment of your home. Recommit to following the first three priorities of a Holy Catholic Marriage. Live love the way your spouse needs it lived. LISTEN to your spouse with love and acceptance.

Live your love for God through reconciliation, individual and couple prayer.

Live your love for your spouse by listening and serving.

Live your love for your children by providing patience and attention.

If both spouses commit to this gentle behavior, home life will improve, become healthier and more loving. Just think of how precious your marriage would be if you lived love, peace, support, patience, forgiveness, humility, self-denial and service. As you grow to be the spouse and parent God expects you to be, ask your beloved to be patient as you work at getting "unstuck" to reduce the arguing. Finally, pray the rosary daily, asking Blessed Mother to soften your personality.

Fear

"There is no fear in love, but perfect love casts out fear. For fear has to do with punishment, and he who fears is not perfected in love. We love, because he first loved us" (1Jn 4:18-19).

Sin blinds us to truth. It can make us fearful and lead us to shift the blame to someone or something else, reality taking a backseat to perception. Although there is no fear in love, when trust and respect are injured, love breaks down and fear takes over.

One tactic used by Satan is to manipulate each spouse into perceiving their beloved as the problem. Believing they have been wronged, neither is willing to accept or take responsibility. When there is an issue, the husband says it is his wife's fault while the wife says it is her husband's fault. They may each suspect they are wrong but rather than be viewed as such, each defends themselves by criticizing and blaming the other. Now, reality not only takes a back seat to perception but is completely overwhelmed by it!

When a couple comes to us for mentoring, in a last-ditch effort to save what is left of their relationship, sometimes they each tell very different stories. Each spouse wants to win us over to prove they are right and their spouse is wrong. They perceive themselves as the innocent victim and their beloved as the crazed villain. The plot of each of their stories is based on their individual perceptions, some of which may conform to reality, some of which may not. Often, the goal is for us to sympathize with them, sometimes to encourage us to perceive them as a victim and other times just have us accept they are right and their spouse is wrong. As Gary has so often remarked, "You know, I hear you both and I'm hearing two completely different stories. Without watching the video, I can't say whose narration is accurate!" This is not very different from several people witnessing an automobile accident and having differing versions overlapping with elements of reality or an art class of twenty people rendering their version of an apple resulting in twenty different visual interpretations! Sometimes perceptions conform to reality and sometimes they do not; it is easy for confusion to reign.

If there is any single biblical passage that sows the seeds of misperception and confusion among husbands and wives, as well as frustration and resentment, it is in St. Paul's Letter to the Colossians where he says, *"Wives, be subject to your husbands, as is fitting in the Lord"* (Col 3:18). Husbands, some of whom have little knowledge of Scripture, have somehow miraculously memorized this quote, repeating it to their wives, especially in the middle of a disagreement!

If we genuinely want to understand what St. Paul is saying, it is necessary to read his entire letter. That means a sincere reading and understanding of Chapter Three: *"Put on then, as God's chosen ones, holy and beloved, compassion, kindness, lowliness, meekness, and patience, forbearing one another and, if one has a complaint against another, forgiving each other; as the Lord has forgiven you, so you must also forgive. And over all these put on love, which binds everything together in perfect harmony. And let the peace of Christ rule in your hearts . . . and be thankful . . . wives, be subject to your husbands, as is fitting in the Lord. Husbands, love your wives, and do not be harsh with them . . . the wrongdoer will be paid back for the wrong he has done, and there is no partiality"* (Col 3:12-15, 18-19, 25). St. Paul is not denigrating wives but laying the groundwork for strong, healthy marriages. St. Paul writes similarly in his Letter to the Ephesians where he says, *"Be subject to one another out of reverence for Christ. Wives, be subject to your husbands, as to the Lord . . . husbands, love your wives, as Christ loved the Church and gave himself up for her . . . husbands should love their wives as their own bodies. He who loves his wife loves himself"* (Eph 5:21-22, 25, 28).

St. Paul traveled extensively in what is today Israel, Turkey, Greece, Malta and Italy. Whether he was speaking or writing to the Corinthians, Ephesians, Romans or Colossians, it is clear husbands and wives have struggled to fully understand their roles for two thousand years! In his Letters, St. Paul is reiterating the words of Jesus who told us to love one another as He loves us. When we stop trying to control and change our spouse but just listen and love, we will have a healthy marriage. A Catholic marriage is about husbands and wives being subject to each other and dying to their determination that each accept their perceptions as "absolute truth."

> **When we fear we may be:**
> • wrong
> • hurt
> • under attack
> • appear weak or deficient
> **We become defensive.**

Fear is Satan's weapon. It is not from God because He is perfect love. Satan uses fear as a tool to divide husbands and wives. Because of fear, we become defensive, feeling easily misunderstood, wronged or unfairly judged. We blame our spouse for the hurt, our relationship becomes divided and destruction follows. We become the weak, blindsided pawn in Satan's scheme to destroy our marriage and prove that love is not possible, that neither love nor God exist.

While on a hike, if we saw a sign warning us, "Quicksand! Stay on the path, don't leave it!" chances are we would be very careful. Well, there are quicksand moments in every marriage, times where emotions can be out of control. Avoid these quicksand moments at all costs! We must remain aware of where we tread and avoid arguing when stressed, hungry, exhausted or feeling rushed because these conditions easily lead to toxic, unhealthy situations.

Other toxic, unhealthy situations can result when we feel:
- Unloved, misunderstood or simply not listened to.
- Unimportant because our spouse is busy with electronics, friends or work, failing to make time for us.
- Our wants and needs are unimportant because we have asked for changes that have failed to occur.
- Our spouse gives us very little attention but freely lavishes time and attention on others.
- Our spouse does not respect or value us.

The more our spouse feels loved, appreciated and encouraged, the fewer disagreements and arguments will occur. Fear of rejection and being misunderstood will disintegrate the more we love our spouse. It is natural to feel defensive when attacked but when we speak in a voice that is neither condemning or condescending, our spouse's need to feel defensive will decrease. We can begin by living our love for our beloved through daily reassurance of our love and commitment. When there is an issue, we can approach it without blame or accusation, asking questions to gather more information leading to understanding. We can take the fight out of the issue by reminding ourselves not to take the present disagreement or argument personally but to see it as an opportunity to work together in an objective, rather than emotionally critical manner. Always problem solve with love, courtesy and respect.

Simple but effective questions and statements:

- "I love you so much, and I want us to get through this disagreement quickly so we can go back to being kind and loving to each other."
- "Tell me what went wrong just now. What did I say to hurt or offend you?"
- "How did we get off track? Was it something I said or did?"
- "I need you to please explain what I said that you didn't agree with or that hurt you. You know I would never knowingly hurt you. If you tell me what I did, I will be sure it doesn't happen again."

These seemingly simple, yet effective questions and statements open the door to communication instead of criticizing, blaming, accusing and arguing. In this way, no one loses and becomes fearful of being attacked.

Share this with your spouse and live your *legacy of love*. When strife enters your marriage, first stop, take a deep breath and verbally assess conditions asking, "What's going on? What's really going on? Who's entered the room? Who wants to destroy our marriage?" Are you going to become hurt, angry or argue to prove your point, be the "winner" and cling to your perceptions? Or, are you going to examine the situation, rise above it and realize that you are being duped into blaming each other, into experiencing hurt feelings and into attacking each other by Satan? Immediately, turn to each other, pray and ask God for the strength and grace to move beyond the argument to once again love and serve each other.

Stiff-Necked, Stubborn and Prideful

"But they and our fathers acted presumptuously and stiffened their neck and did not obey your commandments; they refused to obey, and were not mindful of the wonders which you performed among them; but they stiffened their neck and appointed a leader to return to their bondage in Egypt" (Neh 9:16-17).

We hear about the Scribes and Pharisees being "stiff-necked," clinging to their preconceived ideas about who the Messiah would be and how He would act. Smug in their thinking, they completely missed Jesus when He stood before them. Their sin of jealousy and pride led them unwittingly to fulfill the prophesy: *"The stone which the builders rejected has become the cornerstone"* (Ps 118:22). Blinded and deceived, they were unable to recognize the Son of God in Jesus, whom they had long awaited. Satan duped them with pride, whispering in their hearts they were smart and learned while Jesus was uneducated and a young upstart, just one of many such men looking for a following. Satan convinced their hard hearts they were the true leaders! Preying on their stiff-necked personalities, Satan hatched his plan to destroy God's Son.

Satan cannot love: he can only hate. There is no truth in him: he is the great deceiver. His prideful, manipulative lies are meant to destroy truth, love, faith and all humanity. Prideful Satan

176

whispers in our hearts how smart we are and how others know or understand less than we do. He leads us to believe we see the big picture and others do not. He whispers to us not to worry about the Seven Deadly Sins while continually replaying those we are most susceptible to in our heads and hearts. Satan is most successful when we act upon those deadly sins. We become so sure of our ideas and so congratulatory about our thought processes that we become absolutely certain we are right and everyone else is wrong! As with the Israelites, we are ever so close to being taken back to slavery and death.

When we become closed, hardhearted, selfish and stubborn, our spouse cannot connect with us because we refuse to listen. We are blind, accepting lies because we want to embrace a favorite sin and do not care what our spouse thinks. We may not intend to but we turn away from love and truth toward self-deception, believing it is all right to ignore God and spouse to do as we please. This selfish thinking can lead to selfish behavior, destroying love and marriage.

The stubborn, blind, stiff-necked person says:

- "Scripture is old-school, I can interpret it my way."
- "I'm a good person, the Church doesn't know everything. I can believe what I want."
- "No one will tell me what to do or what to believe."
- "This is my body and my life and I'm in charge."
- "I can do as I please and just not tell my spouse."
- "I know what I'm doing."
- "God and the Church need to stay out of my business."
- "My spouse doesn't really love or respect me, so I don't need to love or respect them."
- "I'm an adult. Pornography or flirting isn't a sin for me. I'll be fine."

These are Satan's favorite hooks to dupe us. He uses these and more to fit our personality and weaknesses. We may think we are doing our will but we are really doing the bidding of Satan who has blinded us to the love of Jesus. We can give our free will to God or Satan. It is up to us.

Teetering on the brink of evil desires and ideas, we look for reasons and rationalize our actions to sin. Satan, ever-obliging, will say, "Make your own rules, Jesus was two thousand years ago. He's in the past, this is now. The old mentality doesn't work anymore." Really? Sin is sin. There is no time or age requirement on sin. Whether we are fifteen or fifty, whenever we commit sin . . . it is still sin.

Why should we listen to Jesus and His Church? Because, Jesus said He is God and proved it by fulfilling over two thousand years of prophesy, pointing to very specific things about His birth, life, death and resurrection. After His resurrection, He remained on earth while five hundred "brothers" witnessed Him walking, talking and eating. The Church He founded, although persecuted for nearly 300 years, grew and grew. It remains strong and continues to grow. Our Catholic Church has produced great Saints who, like Jesus, have given their lives to others in heroic love and obedience to God. In considering Jesus' birth, life and death, together with the persecution and growth of His Church and its' stunning accomplishments, it sounds ridiculous to say, "I know better than Jesus and His Church." Will any of us be remembered in two thousand years? Were we foretold? Are people willing to die for us? Will great cathedrals be built in our name? Satan does not want us to be reasonable and examine the evidence supporting Jesus and His divinity. Satan appeals to our fallen nature, pride and emotions. When the truths of Scripture and Church teachings are so obvious, why do we listen to this evil entity?

Share this with your spouse and live your *legacy of love*. Satan loves secrets because they drive wedges between spouses. Whenever you feel tempted to do what you want, when you want, run to the Sacrament of Reconciliation, explain the temptation and ask for the needed graces and strength to break your stubborn, stiff-necked, selfish thinking. Your spouse probably has a sense of when you have been tempted or hooked into a deadly sin even though you may believe you are the only one that knows. Jesus knows and loves you in spite of your sin and desires to speak with you so He can remove the guilt and spiritual pain. Meet with Him!

Strategies and Sacraments

VIII

Strategies and Sacraments

The Nightly Goal

*"And whoever would be first among you must be your slave;
even as the Son of man came not to be served but to serve,
and to give his life as a ransom for many"* **(Mt 20:27, 28).**

Sixty years ago, roles were more specifically defined. Husbands worked to protect and provide for the family while wives worked to raise children and provide an organized, comfortable home. Responsibilities were not so much shared as defined by one's role as husband or wife.

Today, many American women work outside the home. Returning home at the end of the day, they begin the very real, thankless job of keeping the home running and the children on track, still doing all the work to keep the family going. It is not done as well as prior to entering the workforce but it gets done, although sometimes with a great deal of frustration and resentment. Children receive less supervision. Dinner is typically very simple or fast food. Cleaning is accomplished when time and schedules permit or turned over to a cleaning service for a fee. For many couples, the sharing of responsibilities in the home remains a struggle. Some husbands readily assist their spouse but many refuse, believing that when they return home their workday is complete. Not true! The proper roles are for husbands and wives to work together as each does their part in the maintaining of the home and the raising of the children.

In a sacramental marriage, we are to serve our spouse and family with a happy rather than a resentful heart. Because the home and children belong to both spouses, the responsibilities of running the home and caring for the needs of the children also belong to both spouses. As a couple, husband and wife are to address the evening tasks together with a happy heart, cultivating the idea of joyfully serving each other and their family. Instead of sitting or relaxing while one's beloved makes dinner, does dishes, helps with homework, finishes the laundry and gets ready for the business of the next day, their spouse can assist. When chores and responsibilities fall primarily on one spouse, that person can feel used and become resentful but when they work together lovingly, kindly and respectfully, marriage and family bonds are strengthened.

The sins of sloth and pride may prevent a spouse from helping. Alberta and I have listened to husbands say, "I'm the head of the family. I'm the commanding officer, I tell people what to do" or "I'm the leader of this home and I'll do as I please!" Leaders need followers; no one is going to want to follow someone who behaves in a lazy, self-serving manner. Husbands, for the sake of your family, roll up your sleeves and help! God loves a cheerful giver: each day give your spouse genuine love and kindness through service. Die to selfishness and embrace self-donation. Why? Two reasons: because Christ came to serve and because He said that is how we are to live our love.

> **Jesus said, "I came to serve."**
> **Satan said, "I will not serve."**

Share this with your spouse and live your *legacy of love*. What is the nightly goal? It is to finish the tasks together, get the children to bed and enjoy each other's company for a few precious minutes every evening. Creating a list, dividing responsibilities, assisting each other when possible with cooking, cleaning, homework and bedtime baths is a good beginning. When the chores are completed, avoid electronics. Head for the bedroom, get ready for bed and be together. Spend time briefly sharing the events of the day and discuss scheduling for the next day or two. However, two tired people should not discuss serious issues, so stay away from hot button topics. Be present to each other and spend a few minutes attending to each other's tired bodies by rubbing a tight neck or tired feet. This is intimacy: caring for each other's bodies, cuddling, reminiscing, dreaming and laughing. Before going to sleep, pray as a couple. If one spouse is more comfortable with praying aloud, they can lead. For years, Gary refused to pray with me. I would ask him but he would refuse and we would argue. Crazy! Finally, I just took his hand and prayed. It took a while but he loves how it opens our hearts to each other. We suggest couples say an Act of Contrition, an Our Father, a Hail Mary and the prayer to our Guardian Angel. Then, prayers can be added for family, spouse, an end to abortion, souls in purgatory, our priests, bishop and the Holy Father. This takes three to five minutes but creates a shared spiritual intimacy with hands, hearts and souls entwined and given to Jesus before falling asleep.

Faithful Love

"Little children, let us not love in word or speech but in deed and in truth" (1Jn 3:18).

Marriage is sacrificial love. It is the laying down of one's selfishness for their beloved spouse. Faithful marriage is the heroic call of love in which husband and wife consider each other before themselves. Thinking and caring for one's beloved before one's self is not easy. However, when a couple begins to live in a truly unselfish manner, they fall more deeply in love regardless of how many years they have been married. Both husband and wife rearrange their thinking, "How can I better serve my spouse? What do they need when they return home? How can I most help my beloved?" Giving to your spouse is not weakness but following the example of Jesus.

We sit with couples daily and hear their spouse is not involved in their life. All too often, we hear sad comments such as, "My spouse no longer cares about what I think, say or do. My spouse is all about what they think, what they need, what they want. My spouse doesn't bother to help me. They just don't care anymore." These are heartbreaking words for spouses to say as well as for us to hear. Before this behavior becomes a habit or at the first sign of this behavior, a spouse must shift into high gear and work hard to reestablish the relationship. Reviving a marriage involves a great deal of time, effort, prayer and sacrifice. We must never forget we are a Sacrament of the Catholic Church and God will bless us for our efforts . . . but we must remain persistent!

We are all aware of our spouse's needs, wants and preferences which drew them to us in the beginning of the relationship. We must once again become the person they fell in love with. Change must first come from us. Breaking through a hard, closed heart takes time, attention, appreciation, encouragement, love and service. We must always remember love is sacrificial. We need to sacrifice those things that take us away from our spouse and address behaviors, attitudes and words they have asked us to change for months or years but ignored because we were determined to do what we wanted rather than what they asked for. Now is the time to change; tell your spouse, "I'm sorry for not being the spouse you've asked me to be. Please let me live my love for you as you deserve." When we dedicate ourselves to our spouse, they will eventually see our decision to live a sacrificial life, that our desire to love is authentic and will hopefully once again turn toward us.

People ask us, "How long will it take to bring my spouse back to me?" That depends on God's timing and grace, on one's sincerity, consistency, commitment to prayer, love, sacrifice and the hardness of their spouse's heart. Keep in mind Satan will do his best to interfere, derail and destroy all efforts to be loving, sacrificial spouses. He hates the Sacrament of Marriage because it is based on love and love is something he does not possess. As we have said, Satan is a destroyer. He cannot create life but only destroy it. Be prepared for battle. Satan will encourage a spouse to stubbornly resist and reject healthy, holy, sincere efforts. Stay the course because this is a battle not only for marriage but also for souls. Make use of the weapons of obedient love, sacrifice, the Sacrament of Reconciliation, Eucharistic Adoration, Mass and the rosary.

Share this with your spouse and live your *legacy of love*. If you have let your marriage suffer by being indifferent to your spouse or not loving them as they need to be loved, pray . . . ask Jesus to give you a clean heart and increase your capacity to love. Train yourself to listen with love to the requests of your beloved to serve more selflessly and conform to the Gospel message. If you sincerely put this into practice, spouse and children will see love in action and all will benefit. Laying down selfishness for your sacramental spouse will bring great blessings to the family and help heal divisions. Refuse to believe this is too hard! Yes, it may be too hard in the human sense but Jesus stands next to you, ready to dispense the needed graces. Ask for His help.

And remember those nine miracle words: "What do you need and how can I help?"

Who Are We Fighting?

"For we are not contending against flesh and blood, but against the principalities, against the powers, against the world rulers of this present darkness, against the spiritual hosts of wickedness in the heavenly places" (Eph 6:12).

This is one of the most important concepts ever expressed about conflict in human relationships: all arguments, disagreements, conflicts and wars are from Satan. Every one of these conflicts has a basis in one of the Seven Deadly Sins. The deadliest of all is pride, which says, "My way . . . my idea . . . I'm right . . . my hurt feelings . . . I won't say I am sorry . . . it's not my fault."

Who wants discord in marriages?

Who wants discouragement and constant questioning about marriage being a disastrous mistake?

Who wants fantasies about being single, doing as one pleases, dating and finding someone better?

Who wants spouses to be so miserable to think they cannot go on?

The answer is Satan, who desires the destruction of God's children made in His divine image, baptized into the Father's family and into Jesus' very life. We are being duped when we fall into his powerful trap of fighting and arguing with our spouse, focused on our own hurtful, angry feelings stemming from self-love and pride. No matter how difficult the situation, couples in a holy, sacramental marriage must remain focused on living their love for God and spouse instead of feeling sorry for themselves. Destroying a sacramental marriage leaves the entire family vulnerable.

Parents know little children become difficult, "flipping out" or "melting down" when they are overwhelmed by exhaustion, hunger or too little sleep. It is similar with adults who become overwhelmed by a lack of patience with too little time to take care of daily responsibilities. As adults, we must become aware of the triggers that set us off. Satan waits, constantly ready to take advantage of these times by pushing us to the limit of our emotional endurance. Think back to the last arguments. What were the triggers? Were there already issues of hunger, exhaustion or impatience? Determine the triggers and share them with each other. Resolve to stay away from any discussion, decision or difficulty when these conditions arise. Simply say, "Sweetie I am in a bad way right now. It's not your fault but I need to eat (or lay down for a few minutes . . . or take a shower) and just feel better before I reenter our life together. I need about thirty minutes."

Even with a willingness to make the necessary changes for a more peaceful life, there will still be times of disagreement, so be aware of the triggers that need to be addressed. However, peace should not be such a high priority that we are willing to shut down feelings. That is not healthy and will eventually erupt over what seems like "nothing." Recently, we were listening to a couple talk about their many disagreements that often erupted into full scale arguments. One situation they related began with a discussion of how to fix the potatoes for dinner. Back and forth they talked about how they were not being heard, about how stubborn and inflexible their spouse was and about how they both felt a lack of respect. Eventually one or both of them would completely lose it as a response to the ongoing arguments. Clearly, it was not about the potatoes! There was another, deeper issue involved, one the spouse did not bring up but had been affecting them for some time. However, wanting to be "nice" rather than "petty" they said nothing . . . until the potatoes become the last straw. Boom, WWIII erupts! For all those little "petty" issues, do not shut down but say kindly and calmly, "I don't like that" or "I disagree but I'm willing to listen to your side. I need to have you listen to me too."

This is communication: allowing our spouse to continue to grow in their knowledge of us and their knowledge of how two need to fit together as one. We are free to express our ideas, thoughts and concerns in a peaceful manner. However, if our spouse feels our delivery is argumentative or critical, that is important to consider. We strongly suggest not using words like, "You always" or "You never" or "You should have" or "You could have." These can all become the beginning of an argument. It would be better to say, "When this happens, I would really appreciate it if you could just let me finish my thoughts, then I'll be ready to listen to yours" or "I feel discouraged (hurt . . . unappreciated . . . rejected) when you say this" or "Next time could you think about this a little more and talk to me before making the decision on your own as that would work better for both of us."

Share this with your spouse and live your *legacy of love*. The enemy is Satan and not your beloved! Cease arguing and place your beloved ahead of yourself. This is tough stuff for just about all of us but necessary for a strong, healthy, holy, Catholic marriage. Communicate kindly. If both of you will, the result will be a more peaceful marriage. Pray together. Attend the Sacrament of Reconciliation, telling Jesus of the sins against love and sacramental marriage that result from arguing, placing your feelings, needs and desires ahead of your spouse's feelings, needs and desires. Never fail to see the big picture!

Healing through Reconciliation

"Truly, I say to you, whatever you bind on earth shall be bound in heaven, and whatever you loose on earth shall be loosed in heaven"
(Mt 18:18).

Saints are severely tested and yet their lives demonstrate heroic love for God and their fellow man. Reading about the lives of the Saints, we understand how they lived the Gospel message as well as their endurance during attacks, persecutions, trials and tribulations. St. Ignatius of Loyola called Satan the Malignant Enemy in his famous, beautiful prayer, Anima Christi. Webster's dictionary defines "malignant" as: "evil in nature, aggressively malicious, tending to produce death, tending to infiltrate." St. Ignatius knew the enemy. He wanted others to be aware of the treachery and long-lasting effects evil can have on us and our families, understanding that one person's sin could influence others and continue into future generations.

When a country goes to war, they study the enemy: their weapons, generals, previous battles, weakest areas and strongest defenses. Understanding there is an enemy and that we are under constant attack, we must fortify ourselves. God's enemy and ours is Satan. As a mere creature, he has no power over God, so he turns his hate and war against God's children. Satan is relentless, conspiring to have sin beget sin, evil beget evil, much like throwing a stone into a pond and watching one ripple after another continue to spread. Each person he can destroy is a victory.

Because we are all easily influenced, one of Satan's tricks is to tempt us to engage in behaviors toxic to ourselves and our families. He encourages us to try things we should not and excuse ourselves with the old cop out, "Everyone's doing it, it's not that bad!" Coaxing us into sin or danger, causing us great harm and influencing others are all part of his insidious plan. How does Satan dupe us and accomplish his evil deeds?

A few of his ways include:

- The teenager who believes experimenting with drugs or alcohol is okay and then drives recklessly, causing injury or death to self or others.
- The girl who thinks her mother's warnings about not taking a ride from boys is silly, accepts a ride from a "nice" young man and is beaten and raped.
- The husband and father who tells himself he is going to

view pornography only one time because of curiosity but returns repeatedly, developing an addiction.

- The wife and mother who tells herself she is going to just have one drink at lunch but is soon drinking more and more, cited for a DUI and eventually struggling with alcoholism.
- The worker who steals small things of no consequence, is caught, prosecuted and finds himself out of work and struggling to provide for his family.
- The husband or wife who tells themselves that flirting with a co-worker, someone on the internet or at the gym is harmless, leading to a secret, extramarital affair and possibly a sexually transmitted disease.

Satan attacks us first by tempting us to sin and then replays on the screen of our mind our sins and the sins of others perpetrated against us. Over and over, these depressing, discouraging thoughts loop through our mind much like the news loops through the stories of the day. These thoughts take their toll, keeping us from the joy God intends for all His precious children. Remember, destructive behavior, chaos, resentment, unwillingness to forgive, discouragement and despair come from Satan, as does the constant replaying of sins with the accompanying chaos of life and family. Yes, the Malignant Enemy will continue to taunt us with visions in our head and dread in our heart. He desires us to continue to experience evil and its effects.

> God has given a great gift—a conscience as our moral compass to discern right from wrong.

Enter Jesus, the Divine Physician, with the healing tools He gave His Church, the only true remedy to help us in our battle with

Satan. When we are overwhelmed with thoughts of the past, filled with discouragement, negativity, sadness or anger, we must run to Him in the Sacrament of Reconciliation. Remember, Jesus breathed on His Apostles, conferring upon them the power to forgive sins. This is the first step we must take in the healing process. As toxic thoughts return time and again, we must return time and again to the Sacrament Reconciliation to rid those thoughts from our head. God has given us a conscience to tell us what we should and should not do. When we do not listen to our conscience and decide to do as we please, guilt sets in. While some call it "Catholic guilt" as a derogatory description, it is really an alarm system from God, alerting us there is a problem to be addressed. Attending the Sacrament of Reconciliation turns off the alarm system.

Non-Catholics and even Catholics who are not practicing the faith do not realize the great gifts of the Sacraments. They ignore the fact that Jesus gave them to His Church to keep us strong against temptation. Those who choose to ignore the power of the Sacraments are easily duped into sin, numbing their guilt with addictions and distractions or continuing to remain anxious over their present sins.

Share this with your spouse and live your *legacy of love*. Be aware of the times you are overcome by negative or sinful thoughts that weigh you down, causing you to lash out at your family with anger or to escape through daydreaming and addictions. When this occurs, run to Jesus in the Sacrament of Reconciliation and unburden yourself of the sinful, toxic thoughts and behaviors infiltrating your life. Receive the healing balm of absolution and then ask Almighty God in this powerful Sacrament to give you the necessary strength and graces to combat them and have a clean heart of love for Him and your spouse.

Getting on Track

"He said to them, for your hardness of heart Moses allowed you to divorce your wives, but from the beginning it was not so. And I say to you: whoever divorces his wife, except for unchastity, and marries another, commits adultery; and he who marries a divorced woman, commits adultery" (Mt 19:8-9).

Is our marriage off track? Do we sometimes feel like it is a train wreck? Are we fighting or just no longer talking? Before calling the divorce attorney, we should think about a few things. If abuse or safety is not the issue, why not explore other options? Most couples believe there are only two alternatives: stay together in a painful marriage or obtain a divorce. Actually, there is a third: address the issues and work on them! No matter how bad or terrible the situation may seem, a Catholic marriage is a Sacrament and Sacraments are powerful. It will take time and patience but marriages can be saved if spouses will remain on course and not abandon ship. No man or woman overboard in a Catholic, sacramental marriage!

Satan wants each and every marriage and so inflicts as much pain and harm as he can. Without realizing it, couples unwittingly cooperate with him. Words, actions, attitudes and deeds bring couples to what seems like the breaking point. Satan wins and we lose when he dupes husbands and wives. He is not going to give up, especially when a marriage may be close to destruction. Yes, Satan wants every marriage and he will fight for it, so we must be willing to fight even harder than Satan to preserve our marriage.

Jesus opened the gates of heaven for us and redeemed us from the destructive claws of Satan. However, we still live in a fallen world where sin abounds and the gift of free will continues to be misused. Satan knows our weaknesses and where to aim his attacks. After Adam and Eve's disobedience, God could have split them up and began anew with another couple. He could easily have banished Eve, took another of Adam's ribs and given him a new wife. Who would have known if God had started over? But, they were not expendable despite their grievous sin, retaining their intrinsic value, dignity and still beloved by God. He did not separate them but instead expelled them from the garden as husband and wife to continue their marriage and learn from their mistake. Now, He had their attention. They would need to learn obedient love for God and work together through the hardships of marriage in a hostile world.

If marriage is not expendable to God, how can we think to throw our Sacrament away? Imagine how angry and remorseful Adam and Eve must have felt. The loss of supernatural grace, estrangement from God and themselves, hard work in a hostile environment together with the pain and loss of their wonderful garden were constant reminders of their terrible disobedience. From that day forward, there has been an ongoing rupture between husbands and wives, each attempting to control and seek dominion over the other. God did not throw Adam and Eve's marriage away nor does He want us to throw our marriage away. Jesus gave us the Sacrament of Reconciliation and the Eucharist to heal our hearts, stay the course and preserve our marriage. However, ongoing, tough, hard work is needed in the fight to preserve love and marriage.

A few suggestions:

- First, remind each other who we are really at war with. It is not our spouse but Satan who will tell us it is no use to try. He will whisper, "Things can't change. Your spouse isn't worth it, you can do better. Don't bother, just move on." Satan will tell us to be mean spirited because we feel hurt. He will tempt us to hurt back . . . do not do it!

- Second, speak respectfully using a kind and pleasant tone, look at each other when speaking, making and maintaining eye contact. Refrain from raised voices, harsh words or condescending attitudes. Focus on courtesy, respect and the willingness to listen. Treating our spouse as we would our best friend certainly seems reasonable and proper.

- Third, take a minute or two and list the blessings and gifts of marriage and family. Share them with each other. God brings each man and woman together to become husband and wife and in most marriages gifts them with children. The children deserve both parents to be present and loving to each other and to them. Recount and share the loving, beautiful memories so dear to both. Treat each other as if you were courting.

- Fourth, attend the Sacrament of Reconciliation. This is the opportunity to share the hurt and pain caused to our beloved. It is also an opportunity to ask for the needed graces and strength to become the spouse our beloved deserves, loving and honoring them as we vowed on our wedding day.

- Fifth, pray together at night as a couple. Recite an Act of Contrition, an Our Father and a Hail Mary. Pray for protection of family and heavenly guidance. Pray for an increase in the capacity to love our spouse as they deserve to be loved.

- Sixth, seek Catholic counseling when needed. Only a Catholic counselor will understand the great power of the Sacraments, appreciating and respecting the sacramental nature of a Catholic marriage. This is not the orientation of Protestant or purely secular counselors. In fact, many secular counselors who do not understand the Catholic perspective of marriage as a Sacrament will tell a couple it is time to find someone else, move on and concentrate on having fun. Keep in mind, marriage counseling focuses on the marital relationship, its dynamics, strengths and weaknesses, so refrain from seeing separate marital counselors. Instead, find a professional each is comfortable with and meet as a couple. It is important for both spouses to attend sessions. There may be a need for individual sessions on occasion. However, personal accountability, clarity and consistency of working a single, coherent game plan suffer when each spouse has their own separate counselor. Because the other spouse is not present to listen and offer their perspective, a husband or wife will focus on all that is wrong with their spouse and portray themselves as merely an innocent victim.

- Seventh, we should not share detailed information with family or friends concerning marital issues or personal information that is negative about our spouse. This can be divisive and dangerous as families or friends take sides. When the marriage becomes healthier and we are once again on the right path, the family may still harbor negative feelings toward our spouse. This will only create more difficulties to overcome. Family and friends may become upset over hearing about hurtful situations and may unintentionally fuel Satan's flame to quit. It is usually enough to just let those concerned individuals know that, like all couples, we are experiencing the highs and lows of marriage and that issues are being addressed.

- Eighth, address one issue at a time in terms of how each has inflicted pain in the form of words, actions, attitudes or misunderstandings. Each of us know what we have done to hurt our spouse and we must accept the wrongdoing without excuses. Apologize! When doing so, we must mean it and ask our spouse what we can do to make amends. Saying we are sorry is essential but not enough. There is also the need for restitution. What does our spouse need us to start doing? What do we need to stop doing? We must do our best to decrease and eliminate those painful words, actions, attitudes and misunderstandings.

Share this with your spouse and live your *legacy of love*. Every marriage will be tested and retested. Heated arguments and disagreements do not mean you married the wrong person. However, they are confirmation that Satan is always ready to step in and derail you, especially when you lose focus and cease prayer, the Sacrament of Reconciliation, Mass, serving and sacrificing for your spouse. As problems surface, patiently, lovingly and without criticism discuss what is divisive in the marital relationship. Finally, pray the rosary together, sincerely asking God for a clean, pure heart to fully love your spouse and your Sacrament.

Problem Solving

"If we live by the Spirit, let us also walk by the Spirit. Let us have no self-conceit, no provoking of one another, no envy of one another"
(Gal 5:25-26).

Single people make their own decisions about how they will live. They come and go as they please and live life on their own terms. When they date, they may take the other person into consideration if they choose but if it becomes a burden or they disagree they can move on. However, when they find that special person whom they feel a connection of compatibility with, they are eager to bend, balance and blend who they are to be more lovable. When they become engaged, they focus on details of their personalities and work together to better listen, learn, accept and compromise. Failure to engage in this process can lead to difficulties, creating issues throughout the marriage over the many decisions each couple must address. These issues range from simple ones, such as what movie to see or what to have for dinner to far more complicated issues involving jobs, careers, geographical moves, financial decisions or health and life issues threatened by sickness.

Husbands and wives make joint decisions about how they will live. Therefore, it is important that both spouses have the opportunity to talk through an issue to be heard and understood. This process can be relatively quick or very time consuming because people process ideas differently. One spouse may be able to make a sound decision quickly and seek immediate resolution but their spouse may want to hear all options, taking time to think about and consider each one before deciding on a solution. Please understand this does not have to lead to a problem, especially if the "quick processing" spouse will be patient. Many times the spouse who engages in the more deliberate process may present ideas that their beloved may not have fully considered. However, the more deliberate-processing spouse is responsible to set a reasonable time limit to discuss the ideas with their "quick processing" spouse in order to reach a solution.

How would such an interaction sound? Ideally, something simple yet effective, such as:

- "Hon, that sounds like an interesting idea . . . let me think about it."
- "Okay, what's your game plan?"
- "I want to do some research first, so let's discuss it after we get the kids to bed."
- "Okay, that sounds good . . . I need to get some work finished so let's talk at about 8:30."

We must remember always to answer our beloved even if it is to tell them we are not sure and need more time. This will prevent us from having to deal with a very frustrated spouse. Setting a time limit will avoid the "nothing's been settled, no decisions ever reached" scenario where a couple feels perpetually stuck, rarely experiencing a sense of closure or accomplishment.

Sometimes both spouses are "fixers." These are people who listen, dive in, take the reins and insist on managing and fixing the situation as they perceive it. They may even fight for their decision to be the one selected and implemented. Disagreements and arguments can be avoided if the couple will decide who takes the reins based upon who has the time, talent, education and dedication to address the issues. This is usually a good solution because there will be times when each spouse's special gifts and talents will be needed for a specific problem. Of course, there are exceptions. If one person has an expert financial background but has very little time or hates balancing budgets, their spouse needs to take the job instead of arguing or putting it off indefinitely. If another is good at gardening but is too busy, worn out and exhausted from their job, then their spouse needs to attend to it or hire someone. In every situation, there is the need for open, honest communication. In a Sacrament, there is no manipulation, hiding of truth or exerting control. Both spouses work with each other, sometimes teaching the other skills or ideas they may not have been exposed to. Learning to work together can be a step toward gaining more confidence in one's spouse and appreciating their ability and education.

However, if one spouse demeans the other because of pride, lofty degree, lengthy education or personal experiences and treats them as incapable of good decision making, then problems will result. A spouse may acquiesce at first but in time may rebel. This can lead to feelings of frustration and anger at having their opinions and solutions constantly criticized as "dumb" or "ridiculous." They may even question why they remain in a relationship when they have no voice. Eventually, they will look for ways to be heard and noticed, if not positively then negatively. A spouse that has been hurt will seek to hurt because they feel left out of the problem-solving and decision-making process. It is not difficult to transition from, "You lack respect for my thoughts and opinions" to, "You lack respect for me!"

When problem solving and making decisions:

Treat each other with a sense of love, respect and equality.

Cooperate by listening and sharing information.

Strive for open, honest communication without game playing to avoid manipulation and control.

Remain focused on the goal of finding a solution.

It is helpful to number each of the possible options "1, 2, 3" versus "my choices" and "your choices." Discuss each option together with possible outcomes and consequences and select the best available option. If that happens to be yours, congratulations! However, the selection is based on the best available option, not the author of the option. Sometimes that will be one spouse; sometimes it will be the other spouse. At still other times, the best available option may well be a combination. It is important to remember this is a process stressing neutrality, objective examination of the options and consequences of each option. Possibly one idea will be easier, faster or less expensive.

The ultimate decision maker is of course God and all decisions need to take Him into consideration. Remember, we are given free will in order to live obedient love in all things for Him. The Ten Commandments, the teachings of Jesus and the Church He founded on the Apostles can never be overlooked or swept aside in problem solving and decision making. Love of spouse means we never lie, cheat or manipulate. During the problem-solving, decision-making process, pray to be open to God and the desire to follow His will. Listening and caring for our spouse and their ideas is often more important than the decision itself!

Many couples find the process of decision-making nearly impossible. Every time they begin to discuss an issue, they end up with arguments, anger, resentment and hurt feelings. The decision becomes, "My way and my ideas which are better than yours" and their beloved again feels unheard, unappreciated, controlled and ignored in the decision-making process. Reread the quote from Galatians at the beginning of this entry about the state of self-conceit not being of God.

It cannot be stressed enough that we are a Sacrament of the Catholic Church. How we, as spouses, treat each other has eternal consequences! Think about that. Petty arguments over daily decisions are of little importance when compared to the eternal consequences we deliberately choose when we ignore our spouse's suggestions and holy needs. Learning self-denial requires God's grace found in the Sacraments, time and perseverance. Love and self-denial are decisions toward mature love. The controlling personality has many ways to manipulate a spouse into getting their way but this behavior is totally unacceptable in marriage. On our wedding day, each of us promised to love and honor. Now is the time to keep our word as proof of our honesty before God and witnesses.

Share this with your spouse and live your *legacy of love*. Listen with an open heart. God may be speaking through your spouse to you. The point is not your will but what God wants from you in the decision-making process. First, He wants you to be loving and generous with each other. Secondly, He wants you to have open, honest communication, absent of game playing, with a peaceful, combined resolution. Finally, He wants you always to consider your spouse, never making a decision that could be harmful or troublesome to them. Always seek God's will. Waiting on God takes patient prayer: pray, wait, listen. He will eventually open the door or perhaps send you down a different path. Either way it is hard to go wrong when you are in God's loving hands. Use the open-door, closed-door decision process. Tell God you have a big choice to make but seek to do His holy will. Ask Him to guide you along by closing doors and opening others to understand and work His holy and perfect will. It takes time— sometimes a great deal of time—but it works!

Listening

"That their hearts may be encouraged as they are knit together in love
to have all the riches of assured understanding and the knowledge
of God's mystery, of Christ, in whom are hidden all the treasures of
wisdom and knowledge. I say this in order that no one may delude you
with beguiling speech" (Col 2:2-4).

Couples who struggle regularly report their spouse does not listen. We can never have understanding and knowledge if we do not listen. Listening is a skill to be learned. The willingness to genuinely listen without speaking enables us to absorb and process information. This can lead us to understanding, which is the purpose of communication. However, if listening is poor, understanding will be poor and the result will be poor communication.

> **When communication breaks down, marriages break down!**

In healthy communication, there are two participants: the speaker and the listener. In preparing information, the speaker must first analyze the situation. We would not begin speaking to a room filled with people distracted by each other. Why then would we start speaking to our spouse when we do not have their attention? We should probably ask ourselves, "Is this the right time? Is my spouse able to pay attention right now or are they distracted by the phone, computer, children, work or television? Is my spouse looking for keys, late for an appointment, hungry, tired from a long day at work or in need of sleep?" Any of these things will make for poor listening and may even begin an argument because of an overload of stress.

Set the stage by asking, "When will you be available to listen? I've some important information to give you that will take about fifteen minutes." They can then respond accordingly: "I'll be done in a half hour and I can give you my full attention then" or "Honey, I'm overwhelmed with this paperwork; let's talk after dinner" or "Honey, I need sleep. I have a huge day tomorrow; can it wait until tomorrow evening?" Said patiently and kindly, these are examples of one spouse sharing with their beloved their immediate needs. Some decisions require in-depth discussions and are not resolved in a short conversation. Lovingly say, "I have more in-depth information about this new issue. Can we make a date for this Saturday, get a sitter and really discuss this in full?"

Frequently, poor listening leads one or both spouses to think they are talking to a wall. It has been said the most frequent type of "intercourse" between a husband and wife is not physical but verbal. Yet, as much as we think we are listening, we are often not listening or not listening well. On a scale of one to ten, how does our spouse rate our listening skills? Are we good at listening before we jump in to give our ideas and thoughts? Do we let our spouse finish their idea without interrupting? Do we take time to repeat their ideas and words back to them for clarification, such as, "Okay honey, let me see if I understand what you're saying: you think we should do this instead of that because..." This helps our spouse, who can then say, "Yes that's exactly what I mean" ... or ... "No, I meant this." For additional clarity, we can ask our spouse why they think as they do in order to better understand their thought process. Listening is more than just sitting down and staring at our spouse while they speak. It is an act of love, making a genuine, concentrated effort to understand what they are trying to communicate. Remember, listening—effective listening—is a skill to be developed that takes time and patience.

Suggestions:

- Work very hard at not interrupting. Interruption escalates a situation, in effect saying we are not listening. If we think we want to interrupt, it is time to take a deep breath and remind our self our only role right now is to quietly listen.

- If our spouse says we do not understand, first tell them we want to. Ask for examples that may help clarify the issue being shared. Stay on track; ask them to reframe their thoughts or to provide another example. Tell them we just do not understand. Do not become frustrated and tell them they are not making sense as that will only escalate into tension, leading them to shut down, withdraw, become frustrated or angry.

- If our spouse says we are understanding, then ask what can be done to solve the situation. Discuss solutions that can actually be implemented. Otherwise, situations will continually repeat themselves because of the lack of concrete solutions grounded in behavioral changes. This approach also helps retain positive feelings about speaking, listening and working to understand because changes in behavior are observable.

- If we have listened but disagree, we can still validate our spouse's feelings. Rather than responding with, "You shouldn't feel that way" or "What a crazy way to think," it would be more helpful to clarify expectations, work at correcting possible misunderstandings and talk about whether there is a solution that will benefit the relationship as opposed to a solution that may benefit only one.

Share this with your spouse and live your *legacy of love*. Find the best time for each to pay attention and listen. Find out when it is important to set "date" time to discuss significant issues. Do not forget as a couple to pray and talk to Jesus about the many issues and decisions of life. He always listens and has a plan for you. Listen to Him speak through the readings at Mass or when attending Eucharistic Adoration. Asking your spouse to carve out fifteen minutes each night to read the Gospels together and listen to what Jesus is saying to you as a couple will create, over time, the spiritual intimacy you both desire as a Sacrament of the Catholic Church. In time, you will begin to fulfill the Father's direction to listen to His Son.

Mind Reading

"Ask, and it will be given you; seek, and you will find; knock, and it will be opened to you. For everyone who asks receives, and he who seeks finds, and to him who knocks it will be opened" (Mt 7:7-8).

Life is not a script as it is on television with witty, perfectly memorized lines of love, understanding and empathy. For most spouses it is difficult to immediately and eloquently express the words their beloved needs to hear. Yet, we all need sweet, kind, encouraging words and if we never or only rarely hear them, it becomes easy to think love no longer exists or that we are being taken for granted. Most spouses will not ask for encouragement, attention or emotional support and are hurt when their beloved does not read their mind. Busy with life and lost in thought, one spouse can easily be unaware of the needs of the other.

On our wedding day, we did not take the vow of mind reading. It is important for us to be observant but it is equally important for our spouse to "clue us in" and share their wants, needs, thoughts and feelings. Open, honest communication allows couples more time to fix a problem and less time having angry words and hurt feelings about a problem that they may not know exists.

In marriage, we must focus on our beloved, retraining our-selves to put their wants and needs ahead of our own. Otherwise, marriage will be far more difficult than it needs to be and can easily become a relationship in which neither believes they are listened to, understood or loved. Achieving true intimacy then becomes very difficult.

We are not supposed to just "know" every emotion and feeling of our beloved. Growing in knowledge of our spouse is growing in intimacy. Intimacy is the deepest form of love in which we know and continue to learn more about our spouse each and every day. As we learn and grow in this knowledge, we affirm and appreciate them for who they are. To know our spouse inti-mately requires us to be aware of them, listen to them and ask questions to learn more about their thoughts, feelings, wants and needs rather than to presume we know all the answers. We will then be in a better position to live our love in a way that is mean-ingful to them. When spouses say they have grown apart, it is because they stopped caring about what their spouse thought and did. Grow together through shared communication and shared experiences. Be part of each other's thoughts and lives.

Are we attacking or lovingly teaching?

Attacking: "I spent my whole day doing the things you asked me to do. I made you my priority and you came home, complained and never thanked me for what I accomplished!"

Teaching: "Hon, did you notice all the things I did for you today? You're my priority and I want to please you. But you said nothing and turned on the TV without speaking."

Attacking: "You ask me to go to parties and get-togethers with you, then you abandon me! I feel like a bump on a log, ignored and unimportant to you. How rude can you be?!"

Teaching: "I'll be happy to go to the party with you but please stay with me so we can have fun together."

Attacking: "What's the matter with you? Can't you see all I do for you and the children? The house is clean, laundry done and dinner is on the table and you don't even have a kind word for me. You come home from work and you think you can have a beer and watch TV while I continue to work and serve until bedtime . . . then you want sex? Are you crazy?"

Teaching: "Sweetie, I need your help with the children, homework and baths. If you can help me get the kids to bed early, maybe we can have time for each other tonight."

Attacking: "When I'm upset you get angry at me, saying I'm too emotional and that I need to grow up. You belittle me and act like an ungrateful, unappreciative spouse. Stop putting me down!"

Teaching: "When I'm upset, it's important for you to remain nice to me. I need you to be calm and not be angry at me when I'm upset. Just listen and try to understand what I think and how I feel."

When we are struggling, we need tender care, hugs and reassurance to remind us how very important and loved we are. We need to know our spouse cares about us and wants to understand how we are affected by specific situations. This seems reasonable enough but our spouse cannot read our mind to know what we need. We must ask for what we want and need in a loving, kind manner.

Over and over, we have said Catholic marriages are a Sacrament. Christ is truly present! Marriage is the most serious of all our relationships and yet here we are . . . all too often . . . attacking our spouse. For the sports enthusiasts reading this, imagine marriage as a team sport. *Not marriage as a game but a team sport.* There is a difference. Now, imagine a team member attacking a teammate and in so doing the game is lost. Wow! The play-by-play announcers would be talking about that for weeks! So, how can we be better teammates? We can begin by supporting our spouse in advance, asking what the game plan will be. We can ask about and be sure of our position and role on the team. We can make certain we have a game plan that we have both reviewed and how we, as teammates, want or need to have it handled. Who will do the talking? What needs to be discussed? What does not need to be discussed? A hypothetical example: At a large, upcoming social event will each of you be drinking? And if so, will there be a limit? When there is the potential for an issue who will say it is late and time to leave?

To repeat: since we cannot read minds, it is important for us to share our thoughts, feelings, wants and needs in a kind, non-critical manner:

- "I could sure use a hug."
- "I'd love to hear you tell me I'm beautiful like you did when we dated."
- "Please let me vent without you getting upset and attacking me. It's important for me to just download my feelings."
- "Sometimes I need to just go for a walk and listen to my music. I'm not abandoning you. Please understand, I just need a little downtime."

Words have weight!

Whether one is newly engaged or married for decades, it is never too late to change unhealthy behaviors. Remember the definition of insanity? It is doing the same thing repeatedly and expecting a different outcome! That is exactly the trap so many couples fall into: married for decades and still arguing over the same painful behaviors that were the source of arguments from the time they were engaged.

As we said, many habits learned from one's family of origin may be unhealthy and derail a marriage. Sulking, screaming, slamming doors, stifling feelings or shutting down with silence are all unhealthy behaviors and not characteristic of open, honest communication. Speaking in kindness to our beloved as soon as there is a problem is far healthier, helps us grow closer and enables us to make fewer mistakes in the future. Our spouse is learning about us, so we need to let them know what we need, when we need it. Asking for help is the adult and honest approach.

Share this with your spouse and live your *legacy of love*. Good communication is built on the willingness to listen, learn and change. Have a plan and discuss, "When this happens, I'll need you to do that." If your spouse has a specific, healthy, nontoxic game plan, then comply so that understanding and trust can grow and healing can take place. Open, honest communication and a willing heart can make for a happy marriage. Be thankful to God for your spouse and their willingness to grow in love! When you are hurt, it is natural to attack, so calm down before speaking. Speak in neutral words that do not sound judgmental or demeaning to your spouse. If you need them to say a certain thing or do a certain thing, tell them what it is you need.

And remember . . . you are not mind readers!

Encourage and Appreciate

"For God has not destined us for wrath, but to obtain salvation through our Lord Jesus Christ, who died for us so that whether we wake or sleep we might live with him. Therefore, encourage one another and build one another up, just as you are doing" (1Thess 5:9-11).

Our spouse is a great gift to us but many husbands and wives view their marriage and spouse as an impediment to happiness. Both say they are being used: men complaining they are only useful for their ability to earn an income and provide a home, women complaining they are only useful to provide sex and children. Their roles continue to be misunderstood, especially in this age of selfishness. However, when a wife understands her husband's vital role as the provider of the family, she can then accept his gift with love, appreciation and respect. After all, the income he provides allows them to survive and their family to thrive. When a husband understands his wife's vital role as the provider of new life, he can then accept her gift with the same love, appreciation and respect. He sees her as a precious gift from God. He is drawn to and appreciates her femininity, knowing how blessed he is to love her and the beautiful children she has given him. Believing our spouse and marriage is not a blessing results from listening to the voice of Satan, who desires husbands and wives to hate and reject their gifts from God.

Negative feelings do not come from God. He desires to build us up and to accept His generosity as proof of His love for us. We are His little children, made in His divine image, given free will to trust and obey Him as well as to love our spouse and children. However, Satan seeks to destroy our understanding of the goodness of God. He encourages negative thoughts and feelings leading to frustration and discouragement, often causing one or both spouses to become vulnerable to sin.

When a spouse complains that work and contributions to the family go unnoticed and unappreciated, it is often a plea for love and acknowledgment. Pay attention and answer with love saying, "I'm so sorry. You're absolutely right. I see what you do and I appreciate what you do in my heart but somehow it just doesn't come out verbally. Thank you for pointing this out and when I forget, be patient with me as I try to become more observant and appreciative." Is this applicable to our marriage? If so, we need to memorize it!

Unfortunately, too many times a spouse's need to be loved and noticed becomes a battleground. Lashing out to the already hurt spouse with angry words and expressions of resentment only serves to "prove" they are correct in feeling unloved and unappreciated. Angrily saying, "Why should I appreciate you? You certainly don't appreciate me" or "I'm not going to thank you for the job you're supposed to do" or "Just because you asked for it, I'll never do it" will only exacerbate the hurt. These comments may seem ridiculous but they occur often. The spouse hearing the complaint is really listening to Satan whispering, "See, why bother? Nothing you do is right. You're unappreciated, how much more of this abuse are you going to take?" Suddenly, the "poor me" spirit enters the relationship, communication of one's needs becomes difficult and the result is deep pain.

Where there was one problem now there are two: the original situation and the toxic reaction to it.

Remember, we did not take the vow of mind reading. We cannot read our spouse's mind and they cannot read ours. We must ask questions to understand thoughts and feelings. A spouse has every right to kindly state wants, needs or feelings but without attacking. Their beloved has the duty to respond, addressing the situation with love and kindness without becoming the enemy. We must remind ourselves discord comes from Satan who hates us and our sacramental marriage. Two spouses who cannot communicate and who cannot resolve an issue kindly are being duped by Satan into destroying their marriage, usually through one or more of the Seven Deadly Sins, especially pride.

Gratitude is a basic ingredient to feel encouraged and appreciated. It is important to thank our spouse for working so hard for us and our family, whether it is job or career, doing the laundry or marketing, fixing meals or assisting with homework. Sadly, there are many husbands and wives who look back on their lives with their now deceased spouse and wish they had expressed their appreciation more often. Since their spouse is gone, they are now responsible for all the jobs and are amazed at all their spouse did without any recognition.

We are bound together by Jesus' divine love and our sacramental marriage is to reflect His divine love. Marriage is not a game or competition. There must never be winners and losers in marriage, especially in a sacramental marriage. To communicate in a derogatory manner so that one spouse loses is a recipe for disaster. Sarcasm, yelling, criticism, name-calling, complaining and disparaging words in a marriage, to the exclusion of appreciation and encouragement, are not part of a holy Sacrament. The world and our toxic culture reject Jesus, His Church and the supernatural character of the Sacraments. Catholic marriages must look, sound, feel and be kinder and more loving than marriages that are not sacramental. If a person has learned to behave in a toxic, critical and negative manner from their family of origin, such communication patterns must be addressed and eliminated or another generation will be injured.

When a couple is not getting along, one spouse must take the initiative and begin the process of change. Change starts with one's self, not with one's spouse. For every action, there is a reaction. If one spouse changes how they speak and behave, their spouse will likely change their behavior and communication patterns. If one spouse, instead of complaining, compliments and encourages with a kind and pleasing tone, it is likely their beloved spouse will not feel the need to defend themselves, argue or shift blame. As one spouse changes, the other will adjust their attitude, thinking and speaking. It will not happen instantly. It took time for the marriage to become disordered, so it will take time to put it right. Satan will cause a major upheaval when there is improvement, so do not become discouraged at his attacks and attempts to derail hard work toward a healthier, holier, sacramental marriage. Remain focused on the big picture, knowing Satan is often behind angry, stubborn behaviors. Jesus did nothing wrong, yet He took it upon Himself to initiate the reconciliation between God and man by suffering and dying on His cross for our sins.

Share this with your spouse and live your *legacy of love*. Be the one to initiate reconciliation between yourself and your beloved. Even if you are not at fault, be the one to apologize for the breakdown in communication and express love for your wounded spouse. God loves a cheerful giver; it is truly better to give than receive. Be the initiator of gratitude and encourage your spouse even if they struggle or refuse to appreciate and encourage you. Jesus loves your spouse and desires you to love them with the same kind of selfless love He has for you. Jesus expects you to genuinely live your love for your spouse because He loves them and gifted them to you. Yes, your spouse is a gift from God to learn to love better! Jesus wants you to treat His precious gift with extreme kindness, appreciation and encouragement. Thank God every day for the gift of your beloved spouse and treat them as a precious gift from God in order to teach you to love more and to love better. Choose to replace criticizing and complaining with loving words emphasizing honor and respect. Jesus gave us the Sacraments out of His immeasurable love and fidelity. Live your love for your spouse through your marital Sacrament. When your spouse brings up an area that needs attention in the relationship, listen and ask what can be done to make things better for them and the marriage. Be a fixer and a doer rather than a rejecter full of false pride.

I'm Sorry

"But he gives more grace; therefore it says, God opposes the proud, but gives grace to the humble. Submit yourselves therefore to God. Resist the devil and he will flee from you. Draw near to God and he will draw near to you" (Jas 4:6-8a).

It is so easy to be proud and so hard to be humble. We believe our successes are due to our ability and clever actions when really they are gifts from God that we take credit for. Our debt to God is huge and yet, we seem to live as if we are doing God a favor when we pray or behave as we should. We have heard people say, "God is in heaven but here on earth I do things my way." How prideful! God is within our heart and He knows us better than we know ourselves. He loves us beyond all understanding. We are to resist

Satan, not God. We are to submit to God, not to the world, the flesh and the devil. We are spoiled and ungrateful children when we do not spend time loving God through prayer, obedience and acknowledging all that He does for us.

Married life is not easy when one spouse is proud and boastful. A healthy, happy marriage requires humility. Serve your spouse. Say "sorry" when your words have injured your beloved . . . and do not use the words again. Think before you speak: "Will this encourage my spouse and be a loving comment or will it be hurtful and discourage them?"

The Catholic Church teaches that most children have reached the age of reason by seven. This means they understand the difference between right and wrong. They usually receive the Sacrament of Reconciliation at this age. This is the beginning of their learning the importance of thoughts, words and deeds and how they affect their relationship with God, family and friends. This early training teaches us to make peace in our lives as we grow into adulthood by taking ownership of our actions when they are injurious to others. A spouse who says, "I can't say I'm sorry" is actually saying, "I won't say I'm sorry," refusing to accept responsibility for a wrongdoing against their beloved. Instead, they blame their spouse for somehow causing the wrongdoing. The refusal to apologize only intensifies the original problem. Pride was at the root of Satan's sin while Jesus lived a life of humility, obedience, discipline, service and love. Who should we imitate? A spouse who apologizes does not display weakness but maturity and strength of character, humility and love. Catholics are to follow these virtues.

Rather than remaining stubborn, we ought to ask our self whether life would be happier if our marriage were more peaceful and loving, each of us growing in intimacy. Most people want an apology when they feel they have been wronged. Well, guess what? So does our spouse! We will free our self from selfish pride, anger, bitterness and resentment by learning to say "sorry" as soon as there is a disagreement. Our spouse will see our love lived for them and respect our strength of character and kind heart.

Share this with your spouse and live your *legacy of love*. Remember, you are on the road to heaven and must practice virtue to achieve your goal. Apologizing for one's faults is part of living a life of love and humility, two very important virtues. Catholics who attend the Sacrament of Reconciliation regularly live a life of peace and joy. Spouses who apologize the minute they offend, live their love for their beloved in a very real way. Begin today to master pride and love your spouse!

Fixing the Pain

"Finally, all of you, have unity of spirit, sympathy, love of the brethren, a tender heart and a humble mind. Do not return evil for evil or reviling for reviling; but on the contrary bless, for to this you have been called, that you may obtain a blessing" (1Pet 3:8-9).

Having a tender heart and a humble mind is the blessing we as Catholics and followers of Jesus have been called to do. It is a beautiful thought but to put it in action and live these words in a difficult marriage will indeed require all the blessings and graces God has available for us through the Sacraments. Love and intimacy are dependent on the use of free will. We must "will" to stay the course, no matter how difficult it is to love and heal our broken spouse.

Toxic families of origin, negative experiences and painful relationships have wounded so many individuals. In some cases, they become emotionally "broken" and turn to addictive or destructive behaviors. Upon marrying, these toxic behaviors are brought into the relationship. Desperately in need of love, they struggle with giving and receiving because of their brokenness in mind, heart and soul. Marital and family relationships are often filled with hurt and pain and require a great deal of work to remain intact or even partially healthy. They frequently feel wronged and hurt. When hurt, their deep-seated wounds take the form of resentment, anger and aggression, resulting in attacks to their loved ones. This cycle may be played and replayed over decades, even a lifetime.

How do we stop the hemorrhaging? Personal therapy is needed but some individuals often resist, deny they own the issue and continue to believe others remain responsible for the train wreck of their lives, their spouse and family. Others live their lives creating and maintaining roadblocks, always giving excuses but remaining a prisoner to their pain. How can such lives and marriages be healed? The hurt feels unbearable and all communication appears futile. How does a couple find their way back to a healthy, sacramental marriage? First, commit to change. Ask each other, "Do we want a happier, holier marriage?" The answer will usually be, "Yes, but I have no idea how to get there." If a healthier marriage is the goal, begin by writing one behavior each spouse would like to see the other be willing to work on changing. Just one! In the beginning, these should be small, easily achievable behaviors. Set each other up for success rather than failure! Write one behavior, maintain an open mind and agree to work on changing the one behavior.

- Do not argue!
- Do not justify the behavior in question!
- Do not be defensive!
- Do decide to make your marriage better by focusing on the one behavior to be changed!

Secondly, write down an infraction committed against your spouse. Apologize for having hurt them. After all, if you broke a neighbor's window you would need to apologize and pay for its replacement. If your spouse feels injured by your words or actions, the same rule applies. Apologize and work out the marital damages. Do not argue over whether you meant to hurt them. It is not about if or when you caused your spouse pain. Instead of arguing that you did or did not cause the pain, just live your love for your spouse by focusing on their hurt and helping them address the pain.

- Do not negate the hurt caused!
- Do not minimize the hurt caused!
- Do not disown the hurt caused!
- Do not insist the hurt caused was imagined!
- Do apologize and sincerely mean it!

The third step is for each to attend the Sacrament of Reconciliation, confessing these and any other sins committed against one's Sacrament, intended for unity, honor and love. Tell Father, "I am asking Almighty God to heal my heart and give me the graces I need to repair my marriage and to love my spouse as they deserve to be loved. I have intentionally and unintentionally injured my spouse through my words and actions." Each must begin the process of changing one behavior at a time, starting with the first one your beloved listed.

If the response is, "No way, I'm the victim here," please remember the woman caught in adultery. According to the Mosaic Law, it was lawful for her to be stoned but Jesus told the crowd that only he who was without sin could throw the first stone. No one did. We are all imperfect. It is important to own the pain we have inflicted on our spouse. We must focus on fixing this most important issue for our spouse, our marriage and our own personal holiness. While working on fixing the problems, be polite and pleasant rather than angry at having to work on change; it will help to continually remind ourselves of the promise we all made on our wedding day to love and honor in good times and bad, in sickness and in health. These steps can bring healing to many struggling, hurtful marriages.

However, some people do carry the cross of a difficult

marriage. Their spouse is so broken that they are incapable of love. Jesus is asking them to live a heroic, sacrificial love every day of their life for their spouse. It is not the marriage they thought they were signing up for but it is the one that Jesus gave to them in order to grow in self-sacrificial love and devotion for their spouse. They can help heal the pain through love, sacrifice, suffering and constant prayer. Will it be a fun, intimate marriage? At times it will not . . . but it will be a holy marriage. We do not take fun into heaven. We do take the good we have done through prayer, service and sacrifice as we strive to live as Jesus lived and by doing so, we have given glory to the Father. Let us be clear: this is tough, tough stuff and resistance and discouragement are appropriate feelings. However, as we have said, it is usually a good idea not to let our feelings run our decision making but instead be guided by our Catholic faith and Jesus' teachings.

Share this with your spouse and live your *legacy of love*. Meeting regularly with a spiritual director may be necessary to address the personal struggle of feeling unloved by a spouse so broken they cannot love. Attend the Sacrament of Reconciliation as a couple on a consistent basis and recite the rosary daily. When there are disagreements, arguments or you just feel like giving up, return and again ask for the needed graces. It really does work because Jesus is working on each of you through His presence in the Sacraments. Be patient! Personal change takes time but through God's grace, prayer and your perseverance, you may just be able to effect change in your spouse and marriage.

VIII STRATEGIES AND SACRAMENTS

Do's, Don'ts and the Weapon of Grace

*"If I speak in the tongues of men and of angels, but have not love, I am
a noisy gong or a clanging cymbal. And if I have prophetic powers, and
understand all mysteries and all knowledge, and if I have all faith, so as
to move mountains, but have not love, I am nothing"* (1Cor 13:1-2).

Every marriage will experience unhappy times. It is during those
times that the promise we made on our wedding day seems so
difficult to keep. Although we strive to keep that promise, we do
not want to "stuff" our ideas or opinions. Bending and blending
these components to support and complement our beloved
spouse takes a willing heart to give in and give up certain aspects
of our personality for love of spouse and marriage. Depending on
the willingness to change, it may take years to mature together as
we grow in patience, self-sacrifice, couple prayer and love. It is a
difficult, difficult process!

The self-giving nature of marriage can make us feel vulnerable. Disagreements can separate and cause division. We can feel
isolated, rejected, angry, bitter, overwhelmed, resentful and experience the desire to leave or remain and inflict pain. When harsh,
angry words are exchanged, the original problem is compounded
into the original issue and the fallout from the harsh words and
unhappy feelings of the argument.

> **New love is fun and exciting.**
> **Romance is easy.**
> **Marriage is hard work.**

There are acceptable and unacceptable ways to address the issues:
Verbal attacks against our beloved spouse are not acceptable;

nor are unkind, negative, personal comments about them or their family. These are sins against our vow to love and honor in the good and bad times.

Loud, raised voices, throwing of objects, threatening and physical actions are not acceptable. Foul language and swearing by taking God's name in vain are not acceptable. These behaviors are a sin against God.

Words such as "always" (You always have to win!), "never" (You never listen to me!) or "should" (You should do it my way, I'm right!) are not helpful and often lead our spouse to become angry or defensive.

Knowing the best and worst times to communicate and discuss issues is always advisable. Mornings when both may be overwhelmed with responsibilities or late evenings when both may be exhausted from a long and stressful day are not the best times to deal with problems and possible solutions.

Blaming everything on our spouse is never advisable. It is important to take a few minutes to analyze the effect of words and actions and how we may be contributing to the present situation. Remaining calm and focusing only on the issue to be solved versus bringing in past mistakes or transgressions can be helpful in calming our spouse's frustration or anger.

Asking how our spouse views the issue and what their solutions may be is helpful. Then ... and only then ... offer another possible view trying to incorporate some of their solutions whenever possible. Always remain solution oriented versus blame oriented. The goal is to create an environment where we can view the issue as external to ourselves and one we can work on together to resolve.

Be willing to apologize: "I love you ... I'm so sorry we have been arguing ... I'm so sorry you are upset."

Although unacceptable ways to address issues may have begun in one's family of origin, imprinted and repeated year after year in marriage, the behaviors are destructive and if not addressed, will result in yet another generation shattered and living in a harsh and hostile environment. We repeat: there is no physical violence in marriage; protection of self and family is paramount; seek assistance of law enforcement, friends, family and clergy and then continue to pray for your spouse at a safe distance.

Consider it hypocritical as well as a double standard to maintain self-control in social situations with neighbors and co-workers but be a tyrant with one's beloved. Jesus was kind to sinners but not to hypocrites. It is hypocritical to be kind and pleasant in public but aggressive and angry behind closed doors. Self-control should not be situational. "Losing it" is the same as turning our free will over to Satan who seeks to destroy all we hold precious. However, the good news is that The Divine Physician gave us the tools to weed out deadly sins. Confessing sins in the Sacrament of Reconciliation is an act of humility and we know prideful Satan hates humility. The sanctifying grace of the Sacraments is like an inoculation against evil. Prayer and the sacramental grace can help all of us rein in anger.

Satan despises Blessed Mother because of her purity, humility, obedience, love and holiness. The words the angel spoke to Mary are among the most powerful ever spoken: *"Hail Mary full of grace, the Lord is with thee, blessed art thou among women and blessed is the fruit of thy womb, Jesus."* So, turn to the rosary, a powerful weapon of grace. When praying a rosary, the name Jesus is spoken fifty times as each Hail Mary is recited. For those who pray the complete rosary every day, this number rises to two hundred times! Focusing on the life of Jesus and on His first and most ardent, faithful believer—His Holy and Blessed Mother—puts Satan on notice that our Savior is here and he is powerless against Him. Mary is "full of grace," lovingly desiring to dispense her gift to all her children.

Share this with your spouse and live your *legacy of love.*

223

Remember St. Paul's words that you can have faith that moves mountains but if you are lacking in love you are only a noisy gong and there are probably no noisy gongs in heaven! Finally, never forget you are the Church Militant in a battle for your very soul. Satan wants you to feel hurt, angry, depressed, fearful and unloved so you will lash out and destroy the love in your sacramental marriage. However, through prayer and the Sacraments you can be gifted with strength, perseverance and grace. Jesus knew those who followed Him would be persecuted with every available tool Satan possesses. Satan cannot "make" you do something but he can overwhelm your thoughts with enticement and discouragement, coaxing you to sin. Please do not allow years to pass without attending the Sacrament of Reconciliation and then, when faced with difficult situations, believe God has abandoned you. God does not abandon us. But, we abandon Him when we stop attending Mass and refuse to turn to Him in personal prayer, spousal and family prayer.

Rebuilding Marriages

"So, if there is any encouragement in Christ, any incentive of love, any participation in the Spirit, any affection and sympathy, complete my joy by being of the same mind, having the same love, being in full accord and of one mind. Do nothing from selfishness or conceit, but in humility count others better than yourselves" (Phil 2:1–3).

Catholic spouses are to be in perfect accord with one another in heart, mind, body, soul and spirit. The result? Complete marital intimacy. If spouses were not selfish, arrogant, critical or conceited, thinking their way and their ideas were more important than their beloved and if they approached their spouse in humility, considering them far more deserving of love and respect than themselves . . . Catholic divorces and annulments would plummet!

Be the initiator of love, humility and respect. It truly is better to give than to receive. Influencing our spouse to change through our love and devotion takes time but when we keep God in the loop of our marriage through prayer and the Sacraments, we increase the flow of God's grace through our sacramental marriage. Sacramental grace is a great gift that is meant to help us live our vows of love and honor . . . even when it may be very difficult to do so.

When marriages struggle, couples often seek professional help. As we have said, working with a Catholic therapist who understands the teachings of the Church and the sacramental nature of marriage is fundamental, while working with a secular therapist who lacks understanding of Catholic teaching can be a disaster. After sessions of complaining, airing numerous grievances and hurts, the secular therapist (who may also be divorced) often suggests a couple separate or even "move on" to seek personal happiness and fulfillment with someone else. Such suggestions are the kiss of death for marriage as the secular therapist fails to mention the divorce rate increases in second marriages to 72%! Divorce is very expensive financially, mentally, emotionally and physically for everyone involved. It makes so much more sense to remain married and address even deeply held and long-established issues that threaten the marriage.

When people do remarry, they may not only bring toxic issues learned in their family of origin but also unresolved issues from their first, failed marriage. Unrealistic expectations, lack of trust and a great deal of emotional baggage from broken dreams and unhealthy experiences are quite common, compounded now on both sides. The need to escape loneliness, the security of an additional income and the ongoing availability of a sexual partner also become very alluring reasons to remarry. However, sometimes there is not a great deal of thought given to the children and the impact of divorce and remarriage on them. We have met with couples contemplating divorce and Gary always asks their thoughts on another person raising and influencing their children by asking, "How do you think you might feel when you call on Christmas morning or on their birthday, only to be told by the stepparent that your child is too busy and will call back later?" Or, he asks, "Have you given much thought to the idea of someone who's a stranger to you participating in the raising or influencing of your children?"

Parents, already at odds with each other, may continue to be at odds with separate parenting styles. When there are two homes, there are often two sets of rules. Often, one parent becomes determined to be the favored, "cool" parent, dispensing with the rules of the other parent. There are also issues of "sleepover friends" that come and go from the parent's bed and the children's lives who may well have their own personal issues. Accusations of favoritism within the blended family can become a battleground for the new couple as each bring children into the second marriage. Perhaps the worst-case scenario is the children's mother teaching and manipulating them to sabotage their new stepmother. This can easily become contentious and destructive: we worked with a kind, well-intentioned woman doing everything for her stepchildren, yet being so abused and maligned that she finally turned to alcohol to deal with the animosity directed at her. So many issues! Why not rebuild the original marriage?

The first step in rebuilding is the willingness to change and place God front and center in life and marriage. Remember Psalm 127, about the house being built in vain if it is not built and protected by God? It becomes a spiritual vacuum open to every vice and negative influence, because we listen to and follow the proud, self-righteous voice of Satan and ignore the tenderhearted voice of Jesus telling us to love and die to self. Satan will win if we refuse to live our love for our spouse, to seriously practice our Catholic faith and cling to the Sacraments. Refusing will leave our house open to every seduction and whim Satan can bring against it. This may happen slowly where ideas and priorities are changed little by little until what is lost is the truth of Jesus, upheld and taught by the Catholic Church. Sometimes this is the long-term result of personal or couple laziness. Remember the old saying, "You get out of something what you put into it!" This is true for practicing the faith and for the self-donation of love and service to our spouse and marriage.

The second step in rebuilding is to engage in serious, honest conversation about personal sins and failings as a spouse, accepting individual responsibility and actions that have contributed to the present state of the marriage. Instead of telling our spouse all they have done wrong, we need to consider all we have done wrong. We are the one who must first change, taking our wrong-doings to the Sacrament of Reconciliation where the priest, standing in persona Christi, is waiting to absolve sins and provide the strength and graces necessary to become authentic Catholic spouses. This Sacrament is truly a powerful cleansing experience and we need to attend frequently, especially when we continue to fall into discouraging thoughts and consider giving up.

Last of all, we must turn off the electronics and focus—truly focus—on what our spouse says. Be quiet, listen and take notes if necessary, making sure our spouse feels listened to rather than feeling alone and disconnected. Then do as they have requested. No arguing, rebuttals or excuses! Make a list of all the important changes they have requested through the years. If necessary, rearrange The Five Priorities to their proper order. Time is made for our spouse by scheduling them first, not last. Many couples make the mistake of placing children, job, sports or extracurricular activities first, injuring their relationship with their spouse. Any disordering of The Five Priorities will place our marriage at great risk. When we allow God to build and guard our marriage, we will be living our love for Him by obeying. Make Sunday Mass the center of the week and give high priority to daily personal, couple and family prayer. Living our love for God and our spouse will protect our soul, our spouse's and those of our family. Today, we all are focused on security and the many systems available. Do not neglect the most important security system of all: following The Five Priorities, living our love for God and spouse, changing personal, destructive habits, receiving the Sacraments, praying the rosary and praying as a couple.

When we believe we do not need to follow The Five Priorities, our lives and marriage will be a struggle with no clearly identified plan for keeping love and our couple relationship strong. But, when God remains our number one priority and we constantly remind ourselves that we are bound together by the Sacrament of Marriage and Jesus' love, we enter more deeply into a relationship with Him. Through Him, we will receive the necessary graces to grow in love and intimacy with our spouse.

So, why not rebuild your marriage? It is not that much different than rebuilding a home. Have you ever seen a home rebuilt? First, the architect sets the plans. Next, the contractor demolishes what will be changed, a very messy process with plaster, lumber, roofing and nails scattered everywhere. Slowly, the rebuilding of the home begins, always an arduous process. Eventually, it begins to come together and after a great deal of time, work and effort, the rebuilding is accomplished. God is the architect of marriage and Jesus is the contractor of the rebuilding. It is time to rip out everything we have done to injure our spouse and marriage. Yes, it is painful and messy but we cannot let pride interrupt the process of clearing out the debris and accepting responsibility for hurtful words and actions. That includes a thorough cleaning out of materials such as pornography from websites, magazines or books that glorify sin, statues of Eastern religious figures and games of the occult. Instead, we can place pictures or statues of Jesus and Mary prominently enthroned in the home and ask a priest to bless our home.

Share this with your spouse and live your *legacy of love*. Ask yourself: do you know better than Jesus what is right for your life and soul? Be serious about wanting the best marriage possible. If you want to buy food, run to the market. If you want to buy a car, run to a dealership. But, if you want to grow in love, run to God! He is love. Want love and intimacy to grow in your marriage? Want to learn how to live in a way that is pleasing to God? Listen to Jesus in the Gospels and the teachings of His Church found in the Catechism of the Catholic Church. We will all die at some point; it could be tomorrow or in sixty years. Be serious about how you live your life of love for God and your spouse, asking Him to build and guard your life, your marriage, your family and the home in which you raise your children. Pray, receive the Sacraments and serve with a joyful heart.

St. Michael the Archangel,
defend us in battle.
Be our protection against the
wickedness and snares of the Devil.
May God rebuke him, we humbly pray,
and do thou,
O Prince of the heavenly hosts,
by the power of God,
cast into hell Satan,
and all the evil spirits,
who prowl about the world,
seeking the ruin of souls.
Amen.

Coming Soon!!

Please visit our website:
holycatholicmarriage.com
for information about Marriage Mentoring
and our weekly podcasts.

CPSIA information can be obtained
at www.ICGtesting.com
Printed in the USA
BVHW031322221220
596062BV00007B/11

9 780578 765730